Drugs and Pastoral Care

Drugs and Pastoral Care

KENNETH LEECH

DARTON · LONGMAN + TODD

£1-20

First published in 1998 by
Darton, Longman and Todd Ltd
1 Spencer Court
140–142 Wandsworth High Street
London SW18 4JJ

ISBN 0–232–52182–4

A catalogue record for this book is available from the British Library.

Phototypeset by Intype London Ltd
Printed and bound in Great Britain by
Page Bros, Norwich, Norfolk

Contents

This book is dedicated to the memory of H. B. (Bing) Spear (1928–95), for many years Chief Inspector of the Home Office Drugs Branch, a man who was much valued, respected and loved by drug users and addicts in Britain.

Preface

> The literature of addiction is highly repetitive, sometimes unreliable, and often based on misinformation.
>
> (Alfred R. Lindesmith, 1947)[1]
>
> Every sentence that I utter should be regarded by you not as an assertion but as a question.
>
> (Nils Bohr)[2]

The first book I ever wrote was called *Pastoral Care and the Drug Scene.* I wrote it in one month in 1969 when I was a curate at St Anne's, Soho, and it was published the following year. For a number of years it remained one of the standard texts on drug abuse for clergy, youth and community workers and for many others who were engaged in what was broadly termed 'the caring agencies'. It was enthusiastically received. Simon Jenkins, then a journalist with the London *Evening Standard* and later Editor of *The Times,* said that it was by far the best book he had come across in the field, and that it possessed a 'rare clarity, brevity and mastery of drug fact and fiction', while Derek Howard, writing in *The Times Educational Supplement,* claimed that it had 'an excellence quite uncharacteristic of writing in this field'.[3] Journals concerned with youth work, social work, nursing, and the churches were remarkably in agreement. But, of course, one of the reasons for this, even assuming that their praise was deserved, was that there was actually very little written material in the field.

Since then over twenty-five years have passed, and I had come to regard that book as part of my past, not something to be revised or rewritten. However, intermittent comments, not least from John Whitton, the immensely knowledgeable former Librarian of the Institute for the Study of Drug Dependence, have convinced me that no single book has replaced my original one. John's encyclopaedic knowledge of the international literature makes anyone's task in writing on drug abuse easier than it would otherwise be, and I am grateful both for his suggestion and for his help in making vast amounts of material easily accessible to me.

Lindesmith's comment from 1947 sadly remains true. Much of the material which circulates on this issue is very unreliable and inaccurate. Certainly in the last two decades there has been an improvement in the quality of the literature available. Yet, while there has developed a massive literature on the pharmacology, psychology and physiology of drug abuse, as well as on psychiatric, social, cultural, penal and legal aspects, and while there is considerable anecdotal material on the work of Christian groups, nobody seems to have attempted to do what I did in 1969: to gather together the known data on drug abuse for the benefit of busy pastors, and to relate this material to the ministry of pastoral care and pastoral theology. However, this task has become a more daunting one. Not only has the whole area of drug use acquired a complexity and an international dynamic unlike that of the past, but my own clarities and conceptual securities have been challenged and shaken by the experience of the last few decades. Like Bob Dylan, I was so much older then: I am younger than that now, and I know less. So I cannot write with the kind of authority which I might have claimed in 1969. At that time, from the small enclave of Soho, one felt like an observer of, and to a great extent a sharer in, a subcultural network whose characteristics it was necessary to communicate in part to the general population. Today the general population is immersed in and affected by the drug culture in a vastly different way. So today, in the words of Nils Bohr many years ago, every sentence that I write should be regarded by the reader not as an assertion but as a question. As a result I think that the present work is more reticent, more humble and more provisional than that of 1970, yet, I hope, retaining what is of abiding value from the past.

My personal background

It is important to say something about my own background within, and perspective on, the drug scene. I first became aware of illicit drug use while living in the Cable Street district of East London at the end of the 1950s when local prostitutes were using Drinamyl as a 'wake-amine', and where Frances Tucker, known in the East End as 'the Queen of Indian Hemp', was operating a well-organised dealing network in cannabis. She was murdered a few doors from me on 11 January 1960. But it was as a curate in Hoxton in 1964 that I first got heavily involved with addiction as a result of discovering that the two sons of my churchwarden were heroin users. Through working with them I soon found myself involved with all the heroin addicts in East London. At the same time, the use of amphetamines and cannabis was increasing among the younger kids in Shoreditch and Bethnal Green, many of whom were frequenting the fairly new discotheques which had sprung up in Soho.

By 1966, work with young drug users was taking up a good deal of my time. Because of this, in 1967, I was asked to go to work at St Anne's, Soho, with a brief to develop work with drug users in the clubs and bars, and with homeless young people. In Soho I was one of the founders of the Soho Drugs Group, perhaps the first interdisciplinary local group of its kind, in 1967, and of Centrepoint, the all-night shelter for homeless young people, in 1969. I have been involved with drug problems ever since, particularly since returning to the East End of London in 1974. Today I chair the Maze Project, based in Bethnal Green, which works on drug education and prevention in the East End of London, and out of which has grown the Marigold Project, working with young commercial sex workers in Whitechapel.

A new book for a new period

The original book was written primarily for clergy and for an existing series, the Library of Pastoral Care. It was later revised as *A Practical Guide to the Drug Scene.* The present work is not so much a revision as a completely new book, keeping the basic shape of the original and incorporating most of the earlier material. However, so much has changed over these years that a revision would have been confusing. So it is a new work, but I have tried to include everything that is still valuable from the original text.

While so much has changed, it is significant, and in some respects depressing, that so much remains the same. Within the last few weeks I listened to a mental health commissioner discussing mental health issues in the East End of London and the conditions in our local psychiatric hospital. The discussion could have been taking place – and in fact did take place – in 1965! Also within the last few weeks I have been meeting with local councillors, youth workers and others to discuss the growth of juvenile prostitution in my neighbourhood, an increase which had been documented in the same streets in a report of 1949. The youth service (or what remains of it) is, in many places, returning to the kind of detached street work which developed in the Elephant and Castle in the 1950s and in Hoxton, Portobello Road, and Soho in the 1960s, though without the resources, the sense of urgency, and the co-operative consciousness which existed then. The terrible years since 1979 have taken their toll, not least in the field of pastoral care.

So I write this book with a sense of *déjà vu* but also in a spirit of hopefulness. As I look back over the last few decades, I am only too well aware of the seriousness of our crisis. In a letter to *The Times*, published on 9 November 1966, I described our experience at that time:

> Those who daily face the problems of the young drug taker are finding the obstacles almost insurmountable: hours and days spent ringing round hospitals for admissions; refusals, evasions and interminable delays; addicts whose condition deteriorates and parents whose hearts are broken; doctors who refuse to prescribe, and doctors who prescribe with almost criminal irresponsibility; and an overwhelming sense of hopelessness and despair among those who know the drug scene closest.

There are times today when I feel exactly the same. Yet, in spite of this, I remain hopeful. Real hope can only arise from a point beyond the recognition of, and confrontation with, danger. It is important too to remember that 'hope is a piece of work, not a state of mind'.[4]

I am grateful to all who helped with the original version, who were named there but should be acknowledged also now. They included Steve Abrams, Don Aitken, Lisa Biebermann, Major James Breckenridge, Fred Brown, Professor Allan Y. Cohen, Caroline Coon, the Revd Dr Henry Cooper,* Alistair Cox, Terence Deakin, Dr Paul D'Orban, Rufus Harris, the Revd Ben Harrison, Joe Havens, Dr Ian Pierce James,* Professor C. R. B. Joyce, the Revd Bill Kirkpatrick, 'Doc Livingstone' (C. J. Saunders),* Kate and Mike McInnerny, Mother Mary Clare SLG,* Fr Austin Milner OP, 'Molly the Quean of Soho' (David Morris),* Rod Moore, Dom Robert Petitpierre OSB,* Wendy Robson, Chris Simpson, H. B. Spear,* Rheta Wall, Anton Wallich-Clifford,* John Wandless and the Revd Frank Wilson. Some of them, marked here with an asterisk, have since died, and I want especially to thank the late Bing Spear, for many years Chief Inspector of the Home Office Drugs Branch, who was a symbol of rationality and humanity in that department to a degree that must be almost inconceivable to people brought up in recent years.

Of these, Steve Abrams, the Revd Bill Kirkpatrick and Rheta Wall have also helped with the present book. In addition I am grateful for help to my colleagues Rio Vella and Trisha Mata of the Maze Project in East London, to colleagues at St Botolph's Project, Aldgate, especially Mary Kneafsey Hanks, Michael Mainwaring and Petra Salva, and to John Whitton, until recently Librarian of the Institute for the Study of Drug Dependence. I am also grateful to Janet Batsleer, Mary Beasley, the Revd Eric Blakebrough, Dr Jeremy Clitherow FPS, Derek Cox, the Revd Louise Dolan, Dr Andrew Herxheimer, Carl Leech, Mike Maguire, Andria Efthimiou-Mordaunt, Dr John Marks, the Revd Brian Ralph, Dr Philip Robson and Dr Denise Yeldham.

Part One

The Historical Background

1

British Drug Use in Historical Context

> First of all I say, as I have often said before, that in the earth are elements of things of every kind: many which serve for food, helpful to life; and many whose property is to cause disease and hasten death. As we have shown before that one thing is more adapted to one, another thing to another living creature for the purposes of life, because of their natures and their textures and their primary elements being all unlike the one to the other. Many which are noxious pass through the ears, many make their way too through the nostrils, dangerous and harsh when they come into contact. And not a few are to be shunned by the touch, and not a few to be avoided by the sight, and others are nauseous in taste.
>
> (Lucretius)[1]

The word 'drug' probably originated by mistake. Arising out of the Low German *droge vata* ('dry casks'), it was used wrongly to describe the contents, though the word 'drog' simply meant 'dry'. Thus it is now used to describe (in the words of one international definition from the World Health Organisation) 'any substance that, when taken into the living organism, may modify one or more of its functions'. (A satirical version of this definition sees it as 'any substance that, when administered to three rats in a laboratory, produces a scientific paper'.) However, the word 'drug' is, in the strict sense, not a scientific term.

This book is concerned with a relatively small number of drugs, those which affect the central nervous system, and, within this range, with a certain number of drugs which have been widely 'misused' or 'abused'. Not all drugs affect the central nervous system, and not all those which do so have become 'drugs of misuse' (the term used, in preference to 'abuse', in legislation). In addition, this book focuses mainly on the use of drugs by young people, who are – contrary to popular misconception – by no means the majority of drug users.

So the drugs with which I will be principally concerned constitute a small proportion of all drugs in use. Moreover, much drug use is both responsible and valuable, and many people would not be alive today had they not been given certain drugs at key moments of their lives.

To stress this is particularly necessary since many people assume that 'drugs' are almost evil in themselves. Many Christians speak about 'the drug problem' in a way which is both misleading factually (for there is no single phenomenon called 'the drug problem') and damaging theologically and pastorally. It is important then from the outset to reject the demonology which treats all drugs as bad or equally bad. Sadly this demonising of all drugs is common, not only within religious organisations, but also among politicians and sections of the media, who sometimes feel that they must appeal to popular prejudice and lack of thought, and sometimes simply use terms loosely but misleadingly.[2] This lack of care in our way of speaking about drugs is one of the major obstacles to rational and sane policies and practice in this area.

The drugs with which we are concerned in what is commonly termed 'drug abuse' or 'drug misuse' among young people (the terms are often used interchangeably though they both raise many problems) fall broadly into four categories. First, the hypnosedatives, drugs which reduce motor activity, slow down functioning, and induce sleep. Secondly, stimulants, drugs which increase motor activity, working in exactly the opposite way to the first group. Thirdly, what are called (according to one's point of view) either 'psychedelic' (mind-expanding) or 'psychotomimetic' (psychosis-imitating) drugs, drugs which change, widen or distort experience. Fourthly, opiates (opium derivatives) such as morphine and heroin, drugs with analgesic (pain-killing) action.

Alcohol and other 'respectable' drugs

I have deliberately not discussed alcohol at length in this book, partly because there is already an immense literature on the care and treatment of those with alcohol problems, partly because, as the most widely available social drug and the one most capable of doing serious damage, alcohol would have required far more detailed treatment than the size of this book allows. However, several points do need to be made about alcohol. The first is that it *is* a drug (in spite of the popular but misleading term 'alcohol *and* drugs'), and it does produce physical and psychological dependence, often greater than do the drugs discussed in this book. It is arguably more physically addictive and more destructive, in both physical and social terms, than heroin, and it is certainly the cause of more illness, more social and personal disintegration, and more deaths, than all the other drugs put together.

Alcohol has a long history of social and cultural use, and its relationship with religion is worthy of closer study. As long ago as 30,000 BC, Isis, the Egyptian goddess, was promoting the use of alcohol, and Babylonian tablets from around 6000 BC show the use of alcohol in religious ceremonies. (The Babylonians had sixteen kinds of beer by 4000 BC!) If we look only at western Christianity, alcohol figures prominently in its cultural life. Much English village life to this day is focused symbolically, and often in practice, on the church and the pub. In medieval England, 'church ale' was one of the regular social occasions. Linked with this were the 'glutton masses' which happened five times a year. Parishioners brought food and drink with them to church, and, after celebrating the Mass, proceeded to celebrate a feast at which everyone, including the priest, got drunk. Indeed there were competitions in some churches to see who could eat the most meat and drink the most alcohol in honour of the Blessed Virgin Mary![3]

Alcohol plays an important role also in Judaism where heavy drinking is ordered at Passover and Purim, yet there is little drunkenness and alcoholism in the Jewish community. Most Jews drink, and children are introduced to alcohol at an early age. There is no mystery about the drug and it is well integrated into social life.[4]

For hundreds of years alcohol has been the most widespread

and most acceptable drug in our society, although there have also been vigorous movements against its use, particularly within the evangelical churches. Some people see alcohol as a drug only of the middle-aged and elderly, but this is incorrect. There is abundant evidence of alcohol's continued, and increased, popularity among the young. Studies have suggested that up to 40 per cent of 14–15-year-olds drink secretly at home without their parents' knowledge. A study of 48,292 school pupils in 1995 reported that 60 per cent of 11-year-old boys and 57 per cent of 11-year-old girls consumed alcohol at home. While there is some evidence that young people opt for other drugs as alternatives to alcohol, the main trend is characterised by addition, not replacement.

Again, we know that fatalities related to alcohol and tobacco put those from other drugs in the shade. Some have suggested that heroin-related deaths occur at the rate of one per week, alcohol-related deaths at one per hour, and tobacco-related deaths at one per five minutes. In 1990 the Home Office Statistical Unit estimated annual drug-related deaths as follows:

Cannabis	0
LSD	0
Amphetamine	2
Cocaine	4
MDMA (Ecstasy)	5
Alcohol	30,000
Tobacco	110,000

In some countries the abuse of alcohol has had very serious effects on population. Thus in Russia, the consumption of vodka has been a major factor in the recent reduction of life expectancy. Between 1990–94, life expectancy among Russian males fell to 57.6 years. In 1997, 43,000 Russians died from drinking bootleg vodka, and the population of Russia fell by 430,000. It is estimated that there are currently 1400 illicit stills in the country, ten times the number of legal ones.

Finally, it is important to keep alcohol at the back of our minds because it illustrates the inconsistency with which people look at various drugs. Most people assume that the best way to deal with this toxic substance is to keep it under some kind of regulation, and that prohibition would make the situation worse, a position which is in sharp contrast with the attitude to other drugs. In spite of the overwhelming evidence of the danger and addictive power of alcohol, few people are committed to abstinence, still less compulsory and enforced abstinence, as a solution, for themselves or for all others, and the distinction between use and abuse is strongly maintained. Indeed the idea of teaching people 'social', 'responsible' drinking, what is often called 'controlled drinking', is warmly advocated in a way which contrasts to the attitude to other drugs, including less demonstrably harmful ones.

It is important also, in considering forms of drug use, to remember that particular drugs may be in use for some time before they present problems of abuse. Thus in 1997 the tranquilliser Rohypnol began to figure in 'date rape' cases in the USA and Britain, with over five hundred women in the USA claiming to have been assaulted after being given the drug. It is important also to remember that fatalities as a result of the ingestion of aspirin and paracetamol are higher than those for all the drugs discussed in this book. In Britain it is estimated that paracetamol is responsible for 160 deaths and 30,000 hospital admissions every year. It is known also to be the commonest cause of liver failure and this has led to calls for it to be banned.[5] However, this view has not prevailed, and most people point to the majority who use the drug responsibly.

Of course, attitudes to drugs vary from age to age as can be seen by earlier attitudes to tea and coffee. According to a former Regius Professor in Cambridge, coffee produces a loss of self-command, agitation, depression, and a haggard appearance, while tea leads to nightmares, alarming hallucinations, depression, and a 'grievous sinking'. 'By miseries such as these', the professor warned, 'the best years of life may be spoilt.'[6]

The substances described in this book, which are often used illegally, unwisely and without proper disciplines or controls, must also be viewed against the background of the use of what are called 'therapeutic drugs', that is, drugs which are used for a healing purpose. In one sense 'drug abuse' is a side-effect of a revolution in medicine, and a central element in this revolution is the use of drugs in the treatment of physical and mental illness. In addition, drugs are increasingly used not simply to treat recognisable illnesses or problems but to enhance the quality of life. The transformation of human consciousness, one could say, is itself an industry within the framework of global capitalism.

What is a drug?

So what is a drug? As I observed above, it is a substance which can modify one or more of the functions of the human organism. Such a substance may be of vegetable, animal or mineral origin, or it may be produced synthetically. Many naturally occurring drugs have been used in folk medicine as well as for pleasure, for thousands of years. Centrally acting drugs in particular have been used for social, cultural, religious and therapeutic purposes. Today, however, the study of drug action and the production of new drugs have become major elements in science. There are a number of interconnected disciplines involved in this field. Pharmaceutical chemistry is concerned with the chemical structure of drugs. The study of drug action is called pharmacology, the source and characteristics of crude drugs is the concern of pharmacognosy, while pharmacy is the preparation of drugs for medicinal administration. Over the last thirty years, the study of 'drug abuse' – itself a questionable term – has also become a major activity, and there are many institutes and research units around the world which monitor and research patterns of 'drug abuse'. One major area of study is that of epidemiology, the study of how diseases are spread. Those involved in this whole area of study include sociologists, cultural theorists, anthropologists, lawyers and philosophers, as well as people from a scientific or medical perspective.

However, as I realised many years ago, as a priest working with street addicts, there is often an inverse relationship between the research data and the media presentation of 'the facts'. The same myths, falsehoods and crude stereotypes are regurgitated, with only slight modifications, over many years. It is important that those who work with drug abusers do all that they can to counteract the prejudices and misrepresentations which help to shape and distort public attitudes. It is an uphill struggle but a worthwhile one.

The literature on drugs dates from ancient times. According to legend, the opium poppy grew on the spot where Buddha's eyelids fell when he cut them off to prevent himself from falling asleep, but it had been mentioned long before this in Sumerian tablets of 3000–4000 BC. Both Herodotus and Hippocrates were aware of its therapeutic value. Hesiod, in the eighth century BC, described Mekone, near Corinth, as the 'town of the poppy'. Opium, from which morphine and heroin are derived, has a significant place in British political history, and in the nineteenth century the British smuggled opium into China, an activity which led to the Opium Wars in 1840–42 and 1856–60. Cannabis is mentioned by ancient writers such as Pliny as well as in such revered texts as the *Zend Avesta* and *Culpepper's Herbal*. The ancient Assyrians used it as incense, while in China Hao-Tho (AD 220) used it as an anaesthetic, mixing the resin with wine.

There is no period in Brititish history when drugs have been absent from our society. There was, for instance, considerable use of drugs, both for medical purposes and for relaxation, in the Victorian era. Cannabis, in tincture of alcohol, was widely used by doctors, and its use was promoted by, among others, Dr Russell Reynolds, physician in ordinary to Queen Victoria. It is almost certain that Queen Victoria herself used cannabis under her physician's direction. As late as 1941, it was being praised by the then Professor of Pharmacology at Manchester University as the best drug for depressive mental conditions.[7] Equally popular were the opium derivatives, and opium-based preparations such as laudanum (produced by Thomas Sydenham in the seventeenth century) were widely used. Heroin, in the years after it was produced, was sold across the counter as a cough cure, while cocaine was used by psychiatrists, dentists and others, and was a constituent of Coca-Cola when it was introduced in 1886.

However, it would be fair to say that, before the second world war, most local doctors used a small range of drugs in everyday practice – in particular aspirin, quinine, belladonna, and the opium derivatives, especially morphine. Most of the drugs which are in circulation today, on both the legal and the illegal markets, did not exist forty years ago. Today there is an enormous range of psychoactive drugs which are easily obtainable without access either to medical prescription or to the criminal market. It is almost certainly correct to say that

> probably more than half the drugs that go down all the throats of the world every day are purchased without prescription from chemists and other retailers by sick or healthy people who intend to medicate themselves.[8]

It is impossible to make sense of the use of illicit drugs by young people without recognising this wider context.

The nature of drug action

How do drugs work? The precise nature of drug action in many cases is still not known, and the precise mechanisms of action of many drugs are no better understood than are those which underly the origins of mental illnesses. The brain is itself a complex organ. It is protected by the blood-brain barrier which allows only certain types of molecule to enter it via the bloodstream, though a disturbance such as a fever might interrupt and disturb the balance. Psychochemicals (mind-acting drugs) act on what are called neurotransmitters (chemical messengers) in the brain, and they take over structures in the brain. Drugs act in a variety of ways. For example, barbiturates induce sleep by depressing the activity of the cerebral cortex. Benzodiazepines increase the effect of a neurotransmitter called GABA (gamma-amino-butyric acid) and act as tranquillisers. Monoamine oxidise inhibitors (MAOs) act against the breakdown of transmitters such as dopamine, noradrenaline and serotonin (5-hydroxy-triptamine). LSD and fluoxetine (Prozac) affect the neuro-transmission of serotonin.

Most neurologically active drugs act as synapses involving many different neurotransmitters which interact, producing many different behavioural responses. As a result the precise action of a particular drug on a particular person cannot be accurately predicted. Drug response is to some extent determined by genetic factors, as well as by dosage, setting and psychological make up. Hence the importance of interdisciplinary work. It has been said that 'the integration of brain chemistry with psychology is the principal task which psychiatry is facing in our present era',[9] and this is true equally for pastoral care. Yet it is very rare to find pastors taking serious account of developments in biochemistry and psychopharmacology in their work with individuals.[10] It is here that the drug culture highlights issues which have far wider relevance, issues which affect the nature of human personality and its links with the environment. The interaction between the person and the substance within a given context, which produces a biological as well as a social and cultural shift, is a microcosm of human life as a whole within its social context.

Research in recent decades has shown the particular importance of serotonin. This substance, one of a number of chemicals within the brain, plays a major part in the control of emotional stability and in maintaining coherence of thought. Drugs may affect it by overstimulating its release, and leading to a depletion of reserves. Low serotonin levels can be a factor in increased impulsiveness, and, given the appropriate circumstances, possibly in suicide. One recent writer has identified our society as a 'low serotonin society'.[11]

Towards a definition of terms

I have called this book *Drugs and Pastoral Care*, and have tried throughout these pages to use mainly the term 'drug use'. 'Use' is a neutral term, and I have tried to be careful in using the more common term 'abuse', placing it for the moment in inverted commas. The term 'drug abuse' comes loaded with presuppositions. 'Ab-use' means bad or harmful use. Of course, few would question that there are many occasions where the use of a drug is clearly damaging to a person or to society, or that such use may dominate, and determine, a whole lifestyle. But the term is often used loosely, and there are many situations where it serves mainly to indicate the personal perspective of the person using the term. Not all drug use, including the use of illicit substances, is necessarily abuse. Moreover, in recent years, the term 'abuse' has come to be used very widely and vaguely beyond the drugs field in a way which makes careful analysis difficult. Often the term is used in a way which stresses personal pathology but ignores or underplays the structure of power relationships which are so crucial to much damage to persons (as, for instance, in sexual exploitation and misconduct). So, while I use the term for convenience, it is important to bear this ambiguity in mind. There is no universal agreement about what is 'bad', either in relation to drugs or generally, and so ideological and subjective judgements are bound to figure in this field. Similarly in some places, particularly in the USA, the words 'addiction' and 'addictive' have come to be used so generally that any specific meaning attached to them is in danger of being lost.

It is necessary therefore to attempt to clarify our use of terms like 'drug abuse', 'drug misuse', 'drug addiction' and 'drug dependence', if only to be able to remove from them the inverted commas. These terms are often used loosely and sometimes interchangeably, writers moving from one to the other in the same account. In this book I shall define **drug misuse** as the *intermittent* misapplication of a drug or drugs (that is, their use in a way which was not intended or which experience has shown to be unwise), **drug abuse** as the *continuous* misapplication of such drugs; **drug addiction** and **drug dependence** as equivalent terms for a physical and/or psychological compulsion to take a drug. The distinctions are problematic, not least because many drugs have no clearly identifiable use. But it is possible to show that many drugs do have beneficial effects on human beings and human society, and that certain ways of using them – excessive intake, compulsive use rather than recreational use, and so on – are damaging. The drug misuser uses a drug wrongly, unwisely, the drug abuser puts it to a bad use, a use which is likely to have long-term harmful effects.

Misuse can of course lead to abuse and both can lead to dependence. It is clear that both the major tranquillisers (phenothiazines) and the minor tranquillisers (benzodiazepines) can produce dependence. For a while there was little evidence of a chronic abuse pattern with an illicit market in tranquillisers or antidepressants, though they figured in adolescent drug scenes from time to time in conjunction with other drugs. The general pattern was of 'therapeutic' (doctor-prescribed) use, accompanied on occasions by unpleasant side-effects and sometimes by dependence. However, as will be shown below, in recent years the entry of tranquillisers into the street market has transformed this pattern in a serious way.

What then do we mean by drug dependence? The World Health Organisation many years ago produced the following definition.

> Drug dependence is a state of psychic or physical dependence or both, on a drug, arising in a person following administration of that drug on a periodic or continuous basis. The characteristics of such a state will vary with the agent involved, and these characteristics must always be made by designating the particular type of drug dependence in each specific case: for example, drug dependence of morphine type, or barbiturate type, etc.[12]

This definition of 1965 superseded earlier official terminology which had attempted to distinguish 'addiction' from 'habituation'. It was pointed out that drug addiction led to a compulsion to obtain the drug, a tendency to increase the dose, a psychological and usually physical dependence, and detrimental effects on the individual and society. Habituation, it was claimed, did not show a compulsion but only a desire, did not show a tendency to increase the dose, showed no physical dependence or abstinence syndrome, and showed detrimental effects (if any) primarily on the individual. But clearly there were forms of severe psychological dependence which affected society adversely, and there were many variations of drug abuse which made these distinctions highly artificial. The 1965 study pointed out that individuals may become dependent on a wide variety of chemical substances.

A criticism of the language of 'addiction', 'addict' and 'addictive' is that it tends to portray the issue in static terms as if 'addiction' were a property of the drug, an essence which somehow inhered within the substance. One needs to bring into play a number of forces – pharmacological, psychological, social, as well as economic, political and cultural – in order to understand patterns of drug use. Drug dependence is the creation of a relationship between a particular personality and a drug of choice within the context of a particular social and cultural situation. Because of this, we need to be very wary of generalisations based on a small range of data or on anecdote.

In Britain until the 1950s there were two prevalent types of non-alcoholic drug dependence, one on opiates, principally morphine and heroin, and the other on barbiturates. Both of these involved 'therapeutic addicts', that is, addicts whose addiction was brought about through medical treatment or through professional proximity to the drugs. Both the opiates and the barbiturates produce an abstinence syndrome, that is, intense physical pain and sickness when the drug is withdrawn. The history of these two traditions within Britain brings us to the point at which the pattern of drug use among young people began to take a dramatic shift.

Therapeutic opiate addicts

> Forty years ago there were no morphinomaniacs, only opium eaters . . . Nowadays the syringe of Pravaz is to be found everywhere.
>
> (Tanzi, 1901)[13]
>
> After careful consideration of all the data put before us we are of the opinion that in Great Britain the incidence of addiction to dangerous drugs . . . is still very small . . . There is nevertheless in our opinion no cause to fear that any real increase is at present occurring.
>
> (First Brain Report, 1961) [14]

Illicit use of opium on a significant scale in Britain seems to have developed in the late seventeenth century. During that century, Thomas Sydenham prepared laudanum, and 'Dover's Powder' was produced a short time after. John Jones in 1700 described a gradual withdrawal treatment for opium addicts. The first Opium War (1840–42) marked the beginning of the spread of opium addiction in China, and in 1906 an imperial edict forbade the growth of the poppy and of the use of opium. In 1909 the International Opium Convention met at Shanghai, organised and chaired by Charles Henry Brent, the Anglican Bishop of the Philippines, and on 23 January 1912 the International Opium Convention met in The Hague, again chaired by Brent. The recommendations of the Hague Opium Convention for international control of narcotic drugs were incorporated into the Treaty of Versailles in 1919.[15]

In the meantime, morphine, a natural alkaloid of opium, had been extracted in 1830, to be followed shortly by codeine, which later became an essential component of most cough mixtures. The literature on morphine dates from 1864, and in 1875 Levinstein first used the word 'euphoria' as a description of the state of well-being induced by morphine. Also in the nineteenth-century the hypodermic syringe was invented by Pravaz. The subsequent history of the opiates is one of development of better methods of extracting and manufacturing purer derivatives of opium, but our understanding of the work of the morphine receptors or of the nature of pain itself remains imprecise. The whole area of pain remains a complex one, and calls for work by theologians and philosophers as well as biochemists, neuroscientists and physicians.

Cocaine was the first local anaesthetic used in modern medicine. It had been isolated by Albert Niemann in 1857 from coca brought from Peru. (Legends describe the origin of the coca leaf in the Andes after the Yungas were exiled there by Khunu, the god of thunder.) The abuse of coca is far more common throughout the world than is that of cocaine. In 1886 Erlenmeyer referred to the danger of 'cocomania', the result of the combination of morphine and cocaine which was to play so important a role in the subsequent history of addiction. In Britain there was little incidence of the abuse of cocaine alone from the mid-1920s until its revival in the 1980s, to be followed, in the 1990s, by the appearance of free-base cocaine or 'crack'. In the nineteenth century, however, while the use of morphine and cocaine grew, the working classes were more likely to use laudanum.[16]

The Harrison Act of 1914 in the United States and the Dangerous Drugs Act of 1920 in Britain were the direct results of the Hague Opium Convention. But they pursued different paths, and, while in the USA heroin became illegal, in Britain it remained under medical control. It is important to stress this as it is still widely misunderstood, even, it appears, by leading politicians. Heroin has never been illegal in Britain. In 1926 the Departmental Committee on Morphine and Heroin Addiction (the Rolleston Committee) produced its report which laid down the principles on which the so-called 'British system' of treatment of addicts was based. These principles, known as the Rolleston Principles, were: that the addict was to be treated as a sick person, not a criminal (in sharp contrast to the Harrison Act), and that the prescribing of the necessary amount of the drug for proper functioning ('maintenance dosage') was a legitimate exercise of medical responsibility.[17]

By the 1930s opiate addiction in Britain seemed to be under control, and this was to remain the general impression for two decades. Between 1935 and 1953 the total number of addicts declined from 700 to 290. They were mainly middle-aged and were mostly addicted either to morphine or to synthetic analgesics such as pethidine. Indeed, as late as 1967, 36 per cent of female addicts were aged over 50, and only 8 per cent of them were using heroin. It was only in 1963 that male addicts exceeded female.

Until the 1950s the picture of opiate addiction in Britain was one of a small and decreasing group of therapeutic and 'professional', middle-aged and elderly morphine addicts, widely dispersed geographically, and rarely in contact with one another. Confidently the British Government reported to the United Nations in 1955: 'Addiction is not a serious problem in the United Kingdom.'[18]

Barbiturate addiction

> But the night is long
> and I am full of tossing until dawn.
>
> (Job 7:4, NRSV)

One of the major reasons for the use of drugs is to induce sleep. Before the nineteenth century alcohol and cannabis were widely used for their sedative (slowing down) and hypnotic (sleep inducing) action. Chloral hydrate, discovered in 1869, and paraldehyde, discovered in 1882, both also having sedative effects, historically followed the discovery of the barbiturates, but they came into medical use first. In 1862 the barbiturates were isolated by Alfred Bayer who named them 'Barbara's urates', probably because he made his discovery on 4 December, St Barbara's Day. The first barbiturate to be developed was barbitone which was not used clinically until 1903. Phenobarbitone was synthesised in 1912, amylobarbitone in 1923, and pentobarbitone and quinalbarbitone in 1930.

The barbiturates are drugs which depress the central nervous system. They fall into four categories: long acting, such as phenobarbitone, used in the treatment of epilepsy; intermediate-acting, such as butobarbitone (Soneryl), pentobarbitone (Nembutal), and amylobarbitone (Amytal), used in the treatment of insomnia; short-acting, such as quinalbarbitone (Seconal), used for those with ordinary difficulties in sleeping; and ultra-short acting, such as thiopentone sodium (Pentothal) and hexobarbitone sodium (Brietal), used as anaesthetics and given intravenously. The barbiturates produce a withdrawal syndrome which varies with the dose. Anxiety, headache, nervousness, tremor and vomiting after eight hours may become more intense and severe up to a period of a day, after which convulsions may take place.

Until 1903 when barbitone (Veronal) was introduced, chloral hydrate and paraldehyde were the most widely used hypnotics. But from 1903 onwards the barbiturates became more popular, and this popularity did not significantly decline with the development of the 'non-barbiturate hypnotics'. The first case of chronic abuse of barbiturates was recorded in 1904 by R. Laudenheimer. In 1906 the Registrar-General reported the first case of fatal poisoning from barbiturates, and in 1908 the first suicide. The danger of physical dependence was noted in 1934, and in 1946 it was estimated that enough barbiturates were being produced in Britain alone to provide 'one sleeping tablet per head per day for a million of the population'.[19] G. B. Adams, who studied an urban general practice in London in the 1960s, reported that 407 patients out of a practice of 10,000 were receiving barbiturates. They were mainly women aged 49–54. Adams estimated that around two million people in Britain were receiving barbiturates at any one time, and that 80 per cent of them were female.[20] They were, at this time, the typical British drug addicts.

Barbiturate dependence was once described, by a famous literary addict, as 'the worst possible form of addiction, unsightly, deteriorating, difficult to treat'.[21] In fact, there have been several types of barbiturate addiction (apart from the use by heroin addicts which will be discussed later), and almost all of them have reappeared in recent years in relation to other agents. The most common type is the patient who seeks sedation, almost to the point of oblivion. The elderly person who simply cannot sleep has been the typical barbiturate user, and some degree of dependence has been common in this group. A different type of addict is the person who wants the excitement of intoxication following tolerance, a pattern similar to alcoholic use. The 'cyclical' abuser would combine abuse of barbiturates for sedation with abuse of stimulants, in the past mainly amphetamine. Desk workers under heavy pressure, entertainers, and nightlife habitués have been examples of this type.

Between 1911 and the 1960s there was a major increase in deaths from barbiturates. In 1962, of all deaths of people over the age of fifteen in England and Wales, barbiturates killed 1 in 441 men and about 1 in 306 women. But in the next decade the situation became more serious. In 1971, out of a total of 3,064 deaths from poisoning, 648 involved barbiturates – 464 suicides and 184 accidental deaths. This was largely due to the fact that during the late 1960s barbiturate dependence spread within the adolescent illicit market, and most of this involved intravenous use. Since then there has been a striking decline in barbiturate prescribing with the consequent removal of barbiturates from the market place. Prescriptions for them in England and Wales fell from 17 million in 1965 to 6.65 million in 1975. In Ipswich, where voluntary controls were established in the early 1970s, prescriptions fell by over 60 per cent between 1971 and 1972. In 1979 barbiturates were added to the Misuse of Drugs Act 1971.[22]

After barbiturates: the benzodiazepines and beyond

Today, to a large extent, barbiturate addiction belongs to the older history of the British drug scene. Their decline has been linked to the pattern of drug research and marketing since the 1950s. Much drug research in the last few decades has been concerned with the area of mood change, stress, depression and anxiety. In the 1950s a wide range of new central nervous system drugs began to appear. Chlorpromazine was synthesised in Paris in 1950 and marketed as Largactil by May and Baker in 1952. During these years too the 'minor tranquillisers' entered the market. Several years earlier, chlordiazepoxide (Librium) had been synthesised, and this was to be the first of a series of compounds called benzodiazepines. Diazepam (Valium) and nitrazepam (Mogadon) came into medical use in the early 1960s. The same period saw the emergence of antidepressants such as imipramine (Tofranil) and amitriptyline (Tryptinol) which appeared in 1958 and 1959. Within a short time these drugs were being prescribed on a massive scale, and by the early 1970s concern was being expressed in some circles about their uncritical or indiscriminate use. In a paper in 1972 Dr Peter Parish described the situation as 'a pharmacological leucotomy on a large section of contemporary society'.[23] The recent role of the benzodiazepines in street-drug activity will be discussed in Chapter Two.

Most recently, there has been considerable work on the flow of serotonin, and this has led to the development and marketing of a range of drugs called 'selective serotonin reuptake inhibitors' (SSRIs). While the use of antidepressants has risen by over 116 per cent since the early 1990s, prescriptions for SSRIs have risen by 732 per cent! This is not surprising, for there has been very active marketing of SSRIs by pharmaceutical companies. The best-known drug of this type, fluoxetine (Prozac) was produced in 1988, and by 1995 one million prescriptions for it were being issued monthly in the USA. In 1996, 5.5 million prescriptions for Prozac were issued in Britain to around 500,000 people. Prozac is being prescribed to children as young as eight, as well as to adults under severe stress. For example, some recent research suggests that primary school head teachers use it to a far greater extent than the national average. The claim – made most recently by Charles Medawar of Social Audit – that Prozac is addictive has been repudiated by the Medicines Commission in Britain, but the case is not closed.[24]

Another major area of interest has been in what are called 'mind drugs', agents which can be used in areas such as migraine, nausea resulting from cancer therapy, Alzheimer's and memory loss. The latter area has led to work on what have become known as 'nootropics', drugs which enhance memory and cognitive functions. There has been continued concern also with dieting, and the appearance of Redux, the first new diet drug for many years, was hailed as both a revolution and a miracle. But it was withdrawn in the USA because of side-effects in September 1997.[25]

All these drugs, and others which are not mentioned, raise major questions, and there are certainly serious cases of abuse of the benzodiazepines, which have to a large extent replaced barbiturates in the area of prescribed drugs. It is important therefore to recognise that the manufacture and distribution of legal pharmaceutical drugs is a major element in the emergence of adolescent drug scenes in different periods. It is not possible to do more than allude to the fact here, but it is worth remembering that virtually all the drugs which figured in the adolescent markets in the 1960s originated with reputable pharmaceutical companies such as Smith Kline & French (now

Smith Kline Beecham), Riker, Burroughs Wellcome, Roussel and Sandoz, and they were prescribed by doctors and dispensed at chemists such as Boots.

Has drug use increased?

> Almost every culture in human history has used toxic chemicals for relief and recreation, but ours relies on these substances most of all. Social scientists note that the pressures of modern life are intensifying as our traditional family structure disintegrates, our cities become more congested, and our environment evolves into a vast behavioural sink. In the future these factors will probably lead us to depend more and more on alcohol, marijuana, tranquilisers and other agents to alter our moods and mental states, and to regulate internal and external stimuli.
>
> (David E. Smith and John Luce, 1971)[26]

It is generally assumed that drug use has increased in recent years, Of course, the market for legal drugs has increased tremendously during the last forty or fifty years. Many substances which are currently being used and 'abused' were not known forty years ago. It is therefore a statistical fact that drug use has increased in the sense that there are now far more drugs to use. However, this is only one aspect of the situation. Many of the drugs which are in current use among young people – heroin, cocaine, cannabis, for instance – have been around for a hundred years or so, in the latter case for many hundreds of years. Estimating the rate of increase in drug consumption is always problematic since the nature and accuracy of data collection and recording varies from one period to another. Whether there is more drug abuse today than in, for example, the Victorian age is difficult to say, but certainly the substances are different, as are the social and cultural factors involved. Some forms of drug use have declined, others have increased. What has certainly increased is our awareness, and our media coverage, of the field.

Of course, the way in which sections of the media focus on drugs is not necessarily related to the size or seriousness of the problems. Often drugs which, while open to serious abuse, cause few deaths, are highlighted, while those whose record of fatalities is much greater, receive little attention. Sometimes epidemics are over-dramatised, while at other times there is complacency and assurances that all is well. 'Number of teenagers taking drugs is gradually declining' was a headline in *The Times* on 8 October 1976.

Research into patterns of drug use by young people has produced varied results, though some features are fairly constant. A study by the Central Statistical Office in 1994 suggested that one in seven teenagers had experimented with drugs. Another study at Oxford and Cambridge in the same year indicated little use of heroin but an increase in 'ecstasy'. A study of 48,292 school pupils in 1995 concluded that 70 per cent of 15–16-year-olds knew someone who was using drugs. A survey by the British Market Research Bureau in 1997 suggested that, while 35 per cent of 15-year-olds had used cannabis, only 1 per cent had used heroin or cocaine. The most recent version of the British Crime Survey, published in September 1997, showed that cannabis, LSD and the amphetamines were still the most popular drugs and that only 9 per cent of people surveyed had used 'ecstasy'. While almost 50 per cent of those aged 16–29 claimed to have taken an illegal drug, only 15 per cent had done so in the past month. A study by the Alcohol and Health Research Group at Edinburgh University in 1996 claimed that nearly half of all 15–16-year-olds had tried some illegal substance, while one by the Schools Health Education Unit at Exeter University, published in September 1997, suggested that almost one in three of pupils aged 14–15 had tried cannabis once. However, of 89,813 young people who contacted Childline for the first time in 1995–6, 835 (0.93 per cent) identified drugs as their main problem.

Local studies too have produced varied results. A study in Croydon in 1992 claimed that 25 per cent of young people there had experimented with some drug, while it was claimed in 1995 that between 10 and 20 per cent of young people in rural Shropshire had used drugs. A study in rural Yorkshire showed teenagers injecting vodka and whisky. Here, while there was some crude knowledge, the level of ignorance was extremely high.

This raises a crucial point which all those concerned with pastoral care need to remember: the fact that young children are likely to have some drugs knowledge, which, while it may be inaccurate, may be greater than that of the adults with whom they are in touch. For example, one study reported that 25 per cent of 4–5-year-olds had some drugs knowledge, while 5 per cent of 6–7-year-olds mentioned heroin and cocaine by name. Another study suggested that some 5-year-olds regarded drug use as normal.[27]

Not all of the research is discouraging. Studies in the USA, for example, suggest that infrequent use of drugs is more common than frequent, and there is some evidence of a pattern of decline. Overall rates of drug use in the USA peaked in 1979 and since then seem to have been declining, although the pattern differs from one area, and from one drug, to another. Some research in England and Wales suggests that drug use here stabilised around 1994–6. Whatever the truth, it is certainly clear that we cannot pretend that young people can ever return to a society without drugs. What is important is that there is, on the one hand, accurate knowledge, and, on the other hand, a degree of maturity which makes the onset of serious drug problems less likely.

This chapter has examined the use of manufactured drugs since the nineteenth century, drugs which have for the most part been used by adults. The closer we come to the present day, the more these agents figure in young people's drug use. In Chapter Two I will look at the use of pills and at the types of oral drug use which have dominated the youth scene since the 1960s.

Part Two

The Main Drugs and Their Effects

2

Pills and Solvents: Patterns of Oral Drug Use

The spread of the amphetamines

> The drugs of this group have the advantage of being relatively non-toxic, addiction to them is rare, and there are no serious ill effects; they may therefore be given to outpatients without undue risk.
>
> (Ministry of Health, 1955)[1]
>
> SPEED KILLS
>
> (Graffito from the late 1960s)

The production of Drinamyl by Smith Kline & French in 1951 in the form of the so-called 'purple heart' may be seen as the key event which ushered in the 'pep pill' era among teenagers. In fact Drinamyl was neither purple not heart-shaped but blue and triangular, and when in 1964 its shape changed to round, it became known by the simpler name of 'blues' or 'French blues'. Drinamyl combined dexamphetamine (a stimulant) and amylobarbitone (a hypnotic) and was found to be useful in a variety of conditions. It was common as an antifatigue and slimming agent for some years before 'purple hearts' entered the adolescent drug cultures. Moreover Drinamyl came at the end of a long period of work on the amphetamines.

Amphetamine, a psychomotor stimulant, causes a lessening of fatigue, an increase in mental activity, and a feeling of well-being. In high doses it causes a rise in blood pressure and relaxation of the muscles of the gastric tract. Associated with these effects will be dryness of mouth, restlessness, headache, irritability and tremor. Very high dosage will also lead to mental depression, increased blood pressure, and some degree of disorientation, hallucination and convulsions.

Amphetamine was first prepared in 1887 by Edeleano, and methylamphetamine in 1919 by Ogata in Japan. In 1932 amphetamine was introduced as a nasal decongestant in the form of the Benzedrine inhaler. It was used in the treatment of narcolepsy in 1935, and of depression in 1936. It was used considerably by the armed forces in the second world war, and by long-distance lorry drivers. As late as 1953, Winston Churchill was given amphetamine by his physician in order to boost his confidence before a major political speech. Amphetamine (marketed under the trade name Benzedrine) was soon followed by Dexamphetamine (Dexedrine) which was found to be approximately twice as potent as a stimulant as amphetamine. Methylamphetamine hydrochloride (marketed in Britain as Methedrine by Burroughs Wellcome, and in Germany as Pervitin) was found to be useful in the treatment of apathetic and depressed psychopathic conditions. Methylamphetamine by injection was used first as a vasopressor agent in surgical emergencies, and this was to remain its main clinical use. It remained for many years the drug of choice in the treatment of post-operative hiccups!

It was some time before the dangers of amphetamine were recognised, although the similarity between amphetamine abuse and paranoid psychosis was reported as early as 1938, and in 1958 the literature was discussed by Philip Connell.[2] At the time of Connell's work, amphetamines abuse was fairly restricted to some middle-aged women who were prescribed it as an appetite suppressant, and prostitutes who used it to stay awake. But a new phase of amphetamine use was soon to occur. The years 1962 to 1967 were the key period for the spread of drugs in pill form among young people in London and elsewhere, while the year 1963 was particularly critical for the mass spread of amphetamines. Although the media attention was focused on Drinamyl, it was not the only drug in circulation. The main drugs used in these years were Dexedrine (dexamphetamine), Drinamyl, and the two capsules of Durophet (12.5mg, known as 'black and whites' and 20mg, known as 'black bombers') and Durophet-M (amphetamine and methaqualone), made by Riker.

In 1964 the Drugs (Prevention of Misuse) Act was introduced to control the circulation of amphetamines, but it failed. These were the years of Mods and Rockers, the growth of the Carnaby Street culture, and of the big discotheques. It was the discotheques in Soho, and later the coffee clubs in London, Manchester and other cities, which provided the early distribution points for oral amphetamine, and this reached its peak in the summer of 1967 when LSD and a range of other pills also hit the teenage market. The main sources were thefts from the drug companies, warehouses and retail chemists, and irresponsible prescribing by doctors. There was no evidence of illicitly manufactured amphetamines in these years.

The Second Brain Report in 1965 described the situation in its inimitably quaint way:

> Witnesses have told us that there are numerous clubs, many in the West End of London, enjoying a vogue among young people who can find in them such diversions as modern music and all night dancing. In such places it is known that some young people have indulged in stimulant drugs of the amphetamine type.[3]

Until about 1968 in London, and until later in other cities, the oral and the intravenous drug takers tended to inhabit separate worlds. For the former, the habitués of the discos and the jazz, blues and folk clubs, the use of stimulant drugs was part of a whole new lifestyle in which rock music and the sense of belonging to a 'teenage' culture were integral elements. The spread of Drinamyl and other drugs was part of this teenage explosion. It had little to do with the world of the isolated injecting addicts of heroin.

The coming of Methedrine and its consequences

However, a major change in the shape of the street market occurred with the increased popularity of the injectible form of methylamphetamine hydrochloride (Methedrine, Burroughs Wellcome) in 1968, and this was followed by increased use of other forms of injectible amphetamine. The crucial role of methylamphetamine in 1968 marked a major watershed in the developing intravenous drug culture. Two London doctors, John Petro and Christopher Swan, were responsible for virtually all of the injectible Methedrine prescribed at that time.

One of them, Petro, prescribed 24,000 30mg ampoules of the drug to one hundred patients in the course of one month.[4]

It was Methedrine which transformed the whole character of the youth drug culture and brought the oral and intravenous users closer together. Since the coming of Methedrine, the drug scene has never been the same. The ritual of injection had become an integral part of the wider youth culture, and was no longer restricted to a small enclave of 'junkies'. It was the spread of Methedrine also which led to increased attention among medical researchers to the dangers of amphetamine use. The British Medical Association set up a Working Party on Amphetamine Preparations which reported in 1968 that there seemed little justification for the continued use of these drugs.[5]

Concern about amphetamine use tended to concentrate on two aspects. The first was the question of psychological dependence, and a number of writers referred to 'amphetamine addiction'.[6] The second was the question of psychosis as Connell had described it in 1958:

> The psychotic picture is identical with paranoid schizophrenia, but, without a lengthy follow-up with biochemical control, only speculation is possible.[7]

Amphetamine-related psychoses usually develop after daily doses of 100 to 500 mg. However, there have been reports of psychoses after only 50mg, while many people have used up to 500mg a day without becoming psychotic.[8] In a study of 74 regular methylamphetamine users in London in 1968, 82 per cent had delusions of persecution, 54 per cent had visual hallucinations, and 24 per cent reported 'meth bugs', little insects which pursued them, a common feature of Methedrine use.[9] With Methedrine in particular, high-dose use became associated with high levels of uncontrollable violence, and the whole youth drug scene became much more violent after 1968. 'Speed Kills' posters and graffiti appeared throughout British and American cities.

In October 1968 the Ministry of Health came to an agreement with the manufacturers of Methedrine as a result of which the injectible ampoule was removed from the retail market. But by this time a significant injecting group existed in the London area, and there was an immediate quest for substitutes. For a time, methylphenidate (Ritalin) was the favoured alternative, and within a short time addicts turned to barbiturates and other non-stimulants which could be injected. Meanwhile prescriptions for stimulant drugs of all kinds declined from 5.5 million in 1966 to 3 million in 1971.

Since those days, the two most important changes have been the spread of illicit amphetamine powder, with illicit 'speed labs' springing up in many parts of the country, and the spread of a range of drugs known as the paramethoxy derivatives of amphetamine (see below; more will be said below also about the increased circulation of injectible amphetamine). In addition, the purity of amphetamine has also declined dramatically over these years.

Treatment of amphetamine use remains one of the most neglected and problematic areas in the whole field of drug use. It has been known for a long time that pharmacological intervention is difficult in the case of amphetamine use. However, some doctors would support controlled prescribing of amphetamine and other stimulants as a safer approach than allowing a completely illegal and uncontrollable market to develop with all the associated health hazards.[10]

Paramethoxy amphetamine and the arrival of 'ecstasy'

Since about 1988 a series of derivatives of amphetamine have become popular in Britain (and a few years earlier in parts of the gay community). They are known as the paramethoxy derivatives. One of these drugs, STP (2,5-dimethoxy-4-methylamphetamine), originally synthesised by the Dow Medical Company, had appeared as long ago as the late 1960s.[11] However, the best known of these drugs is 3, 4-methylenedioxymethamphetamine or MDMA (known in popular rhetoric as 'ecstasy').

Contrary to popular belief, ecstasy is not new. It was first synthesised in 1914 and patented by the pharmaceutical company Merck. In 1953 the US army experimented with it as a drug to disorientate the enemy, and it was used in the mid-1960s as a 'love drug' under the nickname 'Adam'. But it was only in the 1990s that the drug became popular within the UK. By 1995 it was estimated that around 1.5 million tablets of ecstasy were being used each week by up to a million people in the UK, although it is by no means clear that all of the tablets which purport to be ecstasy do contain MDMA. In fact, it is probably the most adulterated drug in the country at present. Much of it is mixed with caffeine, LSD, amphetamine and other substances, and a good deal of it may in fact not be MDMA but MDA, the parent compound. There are an enormous number of types and brand names. One study in Glasgow revealed over three hundred different forms of ecstasy identified by users. By 1994 many workers and users confirmed that it was being replaced on the street market by amphetamine. While reports of its spread down the age range may well be exaggerated – an Exeter study in 1997 found that that only 2 per cent of 12–13-year-olds had been offered it – there is no doubt that ecstasy remains a popular drug among young people.

There continues to be considerable debate around the spread both of the drug and of the Acid House and rave culture of which it is an integral part, and there is much speculation about the drug's long-term effects. There have been suggestions of brain damage, adverse effects on serotonin levels, and of a condition similar to Parkinson's disease. Certainly MDMA reduces the content of serotonin in the brain and damages the nerve terminals of the serotonin system. It works in a way similar to amphetamine though there are also effects similar to those of the psychedelic drugs.

Ecstasy-related deaths in particular have led to sensational media attention, notably the well-publicised death of Leah Betts in November 1995. Earlier, there had been fourteen ecstasy-related deaths between 1988 and 1993, seven of which occurred between 1990 and 1992. Of course, every death is a tragedy, yet it is important to exercise care in response so that a mistaken reaction does not make the position worse. The risk of death from taking ecstasy is probably about 1 in 3.6 million, though some estimate it at 1 in 6.8 million. This compares, for example, with deaths from fairground rides at 1 in 3.2 million. As an editorial in *The Guardian* commented on 18 November 1995: 'Even if the highest estimate of ecstasy deaths is true – 50 a year – this needs to be set against the 30,000 killed in alcohol-related deaths and more than 110,000 by tobacco.' The debate is complex, but it does need to be emphasised that most of the young people who use the drug recreationally come to no great harm. Young people at raves may take one or two 100 milligramme tablets in order to get 'sledged' or 'monged' (high or happy), and it is a small minority who take three to six tablets, a process known as 'stacking', and who get 'cabbaged' or intoxicated to a point of collapse. The main health problems associated with these drugs are those of overheating and dehydration, and this has led to deaths from hyperthermia. With overheating there will be internal bleeding, respiratory and kidney failure, and perhaps neurological damage. Much of the damage is related to the closed environments in which raves have taken place since the government controls on open-site festivals. In Britain, in contrast to some other places, MDMA is used mainly at raves, and dancing generates heat. However, the provision of adequate ventilation and provision of water, as in Manchester clubs, can help to prevent fatalities.

However, there are now more home users ('couch potatoes'), both young people who cannot afford the club circuit, and older people who prefer to use the drug at home. There are potential, and there have been actual, problems with those who take ecstasy alone for self-medication in cases of depression, and this group is very much at risk (though this, of course, is true of other drugs also).

Ecstasy and ecstasy-related tablets sell for around £15 on the street market, though prices fluctuate. They are known by young people by such names as Dennis the Menace, White Doves, Love Doves, Disco Biscuits, Big Brown Ones, Triple X, and so on. While MDMA is the best-known of the 'rave' drugs, there are many others such as gamma hydroxy butyrate, an anaesthetic known on the street market as 'GBH', or ketamine, also an anaesthetic ('Special K' or 'Vitamin K') which made its appearance in 1992.[12]

Cocaine and the arrival of 'crack'

It is important here also to mention the changing pattern of cocaine abuse. Cocaine, like the amphetamines, is a stimulant, but, because for many years it was associated in its patterns of usage with heroin ('H and C'), it is often discussed in relation to intravenous drugs. However, the British pattern of cocaine use is varied, in relation both to the mode of administration of the drug and to the social position of the users. There are heroin addicts who inject cocaine also, sections of the aristocracy and workers in City finance who are more likely to sniff ('snort') cocaine, working-class frequenters of blues parties involving black and white people, and numbers of the street homeless, who also use forms of the drug.

Most young cocaine users now use the free-base form of the drug ('crack'). Crack is a form of cocaine in which the cocaine hydrochloride powder is dissolved in water and heated with a chemical reagent to free the cocaine alkaloid base from the salt. It has been around for some time, though the publicity about it has been more recent. The effect of this form of the drug is very swift: it is effective in ten seconds, peaks in 1–5 minutes, and wears off in about 12 minutes. As with high-dose amphetamine use, there is considerable documentation of cocaine psychosis, and it is generally agreed that treatment for cocaine/crack is a neglected and under-resourced area.[13]

Other stimulants

The search for other stimulant drugs goes on, both at the street and club level, and in medical care. A form of smokable methylamphetamine, known as 'Ice', has become popular for its ability to produce a longer 'high' – eight hours compared with 10–12 minutes from crack cocaine. Other stimulant drugs continue to be used, and in some cases have increased in their use, in relation to specific conditions. Methylphenidate (Ritalin), according to one recent report, is used daily by 3–5 per cent of all children in the USA to increase attention, to calm hyperactivity, and to treat what has become known as the condition of attention deficit hyperactivity disorder (ADHD).[14]

The entry of sedatives into the pill culture

> They staggered and reeled like drunkards, and all their skill went under.
>
> (Psalm 107:27)
>
> Barbiturates top the Drug Killer List
>
> (*Bournemouth Times*, 12 March 1976)
>
> The major Scottish addiction problems are alcoholism and barbiturate dependence among the middle-aged and elderly.
>
> (*Glasgow Daily Record*, 3 March 1976)

The recent spread and persistence of barbiturates

In Chapter One I showed that the problems of barbiturate abuse had largely given way to those associated with other sedative and hypnotic agents. Barbiturate addiction was a problem associated mainly with the middle-aged and elderly. Indeed, it also needs to be stressed that, as late as the 1970s, it was among adult patients, not adolescents, that the dangers of abuse of amphetamine (still prescribed for therapeutic purposes), antidepressants and tranquillisers chiefly lay. However, the spread of barbiturate use among young people became a serious problem in the late 1960s and throughout the 1970s. In 1970 16.2 million prescriptions were issued for these drugs. Barbiturate deaths in England and Wales during the years 1959–74 totalled over 27,000. Most of these preceded the increased use by young people. Suicides from these drugs had already risen from an average of 104 per annum in 1941–50 to an average of 735 between 1958 and 1962. But by 1971 two-thirds of cases of drug poisoning involved barbiturates, and increasingly these involved the young. The peak year for suicides and accidental deaths from barbiturates was 1975 when there were 1,121. After 1975 deaths began to fall, though Tuinal was still easily obtainable on the streets in that year at 25p, and it was estimated that 300 million barbiturates were prescribed in 1976.[15]

Benzodiazepines and other non-barbiturate hypnotics

The most dramatic change in the area of sedative and hypnotic drugs since the 1980s has been the effective disappearance of the barbiturates from the mainstream of the legal drug market place, and to a large extent from the illicit street markets, and the increased dominance of the benzodiazepines. This should, however, be slightly qualified insofar as barbiturates are still prescribed, and it was estimated several years ago that around 73,000 prescriptions per annum were being issued for the 100mg capsule of Tuinal with substantial figures also for Soneryl and Sodium Amytal.

The development of 'non-barbiturate hypnotics', drugs such as glutethimide (Doriden), methylprylone (Noludar), methaqualone (Melsed, Mandrax), and nitrazepam (Mogadon) opened up a new area for abuse of barbiturate type among adolescents. While barbiturate dependence remained a problem mainly affecting adult patients, studies from the early 1970s onwards expressed concern at the dangers arising from the newer hypnotics. In the 1960s non-barbiturate hypnotics, such as methaqualone, had become popular, and a form of methaqualone with diphenhydramine, marketed as Mandrax by Roussel, figured greatly in adolescent drug markets as well as in many cases of self-poisoning. Mandrax abuse was observed within one year of its introduction in 1965. By 1970 Mandrax and Mogadon accounted for one quarter of all hypnotics prescribed in England and Wales.[16]

The really significant shift, therefore, which has taken place both in the field of street drug use, and in the more widespread forms of 'respectable' drug use by older persons, has been in epidemiology. In general the benzodiazepines have replaced the barbiturates in almost every area discussed in Chapter One. The benzodiazepines block receptors in the brain and limit the effects of stress. Developed in the 1950s and 1960s, they include drugs such as diazepam (Valium), chlordiazepoxide (Librium), oxazepam (Serenid), temazepam (Normison), nitrazepam (Mogadon), and lorazepam (Ativan). By 1973 Valium had become the most widely prescribed drug in the world. In that year, in the USA alone 47 million prescriptions for this drug were issued, while around 14 per cent of people in the UK were using it, often having had it prescribed, mistakenly, for depression.

As was the case with barbiturates in past years, the elderly person who cannot sleep is still the typical benzodiazepine user. Such a person may seek oblivion. Withdrawal symptoms certainly occur with the benzodiazepines, and include phobic anxiety ('panic attacks') and, as with alcohol and barbiturates, epileptic fits. Alcohol, barbiturates and the benzodiazepines are cross-tolerant, that is, tolerance to one member of the group produces tolerance to the others. Again, as with barbiturates, benzodiazepines are often used to 'come down' from the use of stimulants. Since the early 1970s undoubtedly the spread of benzodiazepines has taken over the central stage in terms of oral drug use, and an increasing role in the intravenous scene, and in 1995 over 22 million prescriptions for benzodiazepines and tricyclics were being issued.

Of these it is temazepam which has figured most dramatically in recent drug use by young people, and this continues to be the case although the drug was controlled in September 1995. During the last few years it has been selling cheaply on the street market with prices for the 10mg capsules fluctuating between £1 and £4, and there have been similar prices for DF 118 and Valium. Temazepam is known among young users by such names as jellies, or wobbly eggs, and addicts as 'jelly heads'. By the mid-1990s around 7 million prescriptions for temazepam were being issued annually in Britain, of which 850,000 were in Scotland. Most cases of misuse have involved the 10mg and 20mg capsules. Often the capsule contents are heated up in a microwave, or with water, or even by the warmth of the hand. However, once in the bloodstream, the solution can return to a gel and clog up the blood system, thus causing gangrene. A study in Edinburgh of 976 users showed that one in five used the drug by injection, while 54 per cent claimed that they did not know that the drug was addictive. The average age of the users was nineteen.

There is a major street traffic in these drugs. Two million temazepam tablets were found near Heathrow Airport in October 1995. In 1994, 97 addicts died from combinations of heroin and temazepam. In Strathclyde alone in 1994, of 95 drug-related deaths, about half were believed to be linked to temazepam. In the Glasgow area there are more temazepam deaths than anywhere in Europe.

Temazepam is not the only drug of concern in this group. Some years earlier concern about the psychological effects of triazolam (Halcion) led to a ban in the Netherlands and later in the UK. During the 1980s there was a decline in prescribing benzodiazepines, though the street market continues to flourish. The decline in prescribing has been a mixed blessing, and today many doctors are reluctant to prescribe any hypnotic drugs or tranquillisers, and even, in some cases, anti-depressants. As a result, the people who could benefit from the responsible use of these drugs are suffering, while those who misuse them find no difficulty in obtaining their supplies.[17]

Solvent abuse

> This is how it's done . . . They pour the glue into a milk bottle and inhale the dangerous vapours in as confined a space as possible.
>
> (*Sunderland Echo*, 18 September 1985)

A final area for concern is the use of solvents which have been termed 'the alcohol of the young masses'.[18] Indeed one study of young sniffers on a West London housing estate reported:

> Their behaviour appeared similar to that of a group of older alcoholics and seemed to represent an uneasy parallel with being down and out in London.[19]

While 'glue sniffing' is the form of use which has attracted most media attention (since 1959 in the USA and since 1962 in Britain), glues and impact adhesives are not the only types of substance used. Among the others are aerosol sprays, petrol, lighter refills, cleaning fluids and nail varnish remover. The main hydrocarbons involved are toluene and trichloroethane.

Solvent use has tended to involve younger males, often 12–16-year-olds, although some users are as young as eight. They are often living in run-down neighbourhoods, though there has been an increase recently in this type of drug use among older homeless people. Among the younger people, the evidence suggests that this is a transitional form of drug use and does not last. There is no genuine subculture and virtually no jargon. Most solvent users 'mature out'. However, there is no clear evidence that solvent use is declining, although solvent-related deaths have declined since 1991.

From 1971 to 1994 there were 1451 deaths associated with volatile substances, with an increase between 1984–90 and a decline from 1991–4. Of those who died between 1971 and 1989, 73 per cent were under nineteen years of age. Between 1985–91 there were over 700 solvent-related deaths. There are currently around 100 deaths per year from solvent use. One study of 140 deaths between 1971–81 showed that, of 39 deaths in 1981, 79 per cent were aged under twenty, and they were mostly male. The main danger is the use of plastic bags (freezer or crisp bags usually) for sniffing, and this has led to suffocation. In addition, since 1988 there have been more deaths from spraying lighter fuel (butane) down the throat. Sniffing in dangerous places such as high buildings, near railway lines and canals, as well as the inhaling of vomit after sniffing, can also lead to fatalities.[20]

There are many other types of oral drug use, and the scene is constantly changing. Often a pill, tablet or capsule, or some liquid or solvent, which has been around for many years, will suddenly become a focus of attention. Oral drug use is still, in statistical terms, the dominant type, though, as I shall show in the next chapter, injection has become more common among young people over the last thirty years.

3

Needle Drugs: Heroin, Cocaine and Intravenous Drug Use

> Among the remedies which it has pleased Almighty God to give to man to relieve his sufferings, none is so universal and so efficacious as opium.
>
> (Thomas Sydenham, 1680)[1]
>
> There is no good to be done till the habitual cause is removed, viz the taking of opium which suddenly to leave off is (as was shown) very dangerous. Therefore, in order to leave it off safely, you must stop your hand and not increase the dose that is taken, by which means it will come to have little or no effect . . . Then only lessen the 100th part every day till you come to take none at all.
>
> (John Jones, 1700)[2]

Heroin, cocaine and needle drugs

Heroin is one of many drugs which can be injected, and for many years most injecting addicts ('junkies') were injecting heroin, with or without cocaine. It is appropriate therefore to consider heroin alongside the phenomenon of injection. Indeed many observers of drug cultures believe that the mode of administration is of greater importance than the substance injected, and that dependence is as much on the needle as on the drug. Cocaine is pharmacologically unrelated to the opiates, having more in common with amphetamine. However, because it has played such an important role in the intravenous drug culture, as also have the amphetamines, cocaine is included in this chapter in addition to the preceding one.

There are, according to informed estimates, over five million injecting addicts in the world, located in about one hundred and twenty countries. A high proportion of them use heroin. While heroin can be taken by other routes – such as smoking – it has come to be linked, both in the popular mind and often in statistical fact, with the process of injection. Intravenous drug addiction is one of the most destructive lifestyles which can affect human persons, and so the evidence from many places of an increase in injecting is a cause of great spiritual and social as well as medical concern.

Heroin is the popular name given to diamorphine, a form of acetylated morphine (morphine heated over acetic anyhydride). Morphine, a natural alkaloid of opium, was first extracted in 1830, and heroin was introduced in 1874, the popular name being given to it in 1898. It has been available in the UK, at first over the counter and later on prescription, since then. It is still regarded by many experts as the best drug in the treatment of terminal pain. (A recent story on the Channel 4 'soap' *Brookside* may have helped to reinforce and increase public misinformation and misunderstanding of the therapeutic value of heroin.) As was shown in Chapter Two, until the 1950s most heroin and cocaine addicts in Britain were of therapeutic or 'iatrogenic' (doctor-induced) origin, that is, they had been given the drug by physicians for treatment of pain and had become addicted by accident.

Cocaine was isolated from coca in 1857, and is a powerful cerebral stimulant. Once used in psychotherapy, for example, by Sigmund Freud, and by dentists, it has virtually disappeared from therapeutic use. As a drug of injection, it has been linked with heroin for many years, though it is often used alone or in conjunction with other drugs.

The spread of injection among young people

> English addicts are geographically dispersed, rarely in contact with one another, and probably predominantly middle class.
>
> (Isidor Chein et al, 1964)[3]

The recognition of a growing heroin problem among young people in Britain was slow to arise. The Report of the Interdepartmental Committee, best known as the First Brain Report, noted in 1961:

> After careful consideration of all the data put before us we are of the opinion that in Great Britain the incidence of addiction to dangerous drugs . . . is still very small . . . There is nevertheless in our opinion no cause to fear that any real increase is at present occurring.[4]

In fact, at that precise moment the ground was being prepared for a new phase. During the 1950s, and particularly during the second half of the 1960s, the position changed dramatically as heroin spread among the young, originally among middle-class youth. Initially the spread was most marked in London, and, to a lesser extent, Birmingham. The West End of London was to remain the focal point of the injecting drug culture for some years. By the end of the 1960s, numbers of working-class young people were significantly involved, both in other parts of London and elsewhere in the country.

Between 1935 and 1953 the number of addicts known to the Home Office fell from around 700 to 290. From 1954, however, the number began to rise. In 1958 there were 442, of whom 62 were using heroin, and this rose to 454 in 1959, of whom 68 were using heroin. In 1960 there was a drop in the total figure to 437, but an increase in the number using heroin to 94. Unlike the earlier addicts, who were mainly middle-aged or elderly morphine addicts, the new addicts were aged between 15 and 35, and their addiction was 'non-therapeutic' in origin. Between 1960 and 1968 the numbers of addicts rose from 437 to 2782, and the number using heroin from 94 to 2240. Again, the number of young addicts under the age of 20 increased dramatically in these years from 1 to 764.

Almost all of these new addicts began to use heroin illicitly. Between 1954 and 1964 there were only fourteen new cases of therapeutic addiction, contrasted with 4336 of non-therapeutic origin. The spectacular increase continued until 1967 when the numbers of heroin addicts grew from 899 to 1299, an increase of 44 per cent on the previous year, while in 1968 there was a net increase of addicts of all dangerous drugs of 1053 (61 per cent). The number of heroin addicts in 1968 rose to 2240, and addicts under 20 had increased from 395 to 764 (93 per cent), of whom 709 were using heroin. In 1968, 79 per cent of all addicts were under the age of 25.

The 'marked increase in the number of persons addicted to diacetylmorphine (heroin), especially in the younger age groups' was first noted in the Government's Report to the United Nations for 1964.[5] The Interdepartmental Committee on Drug Addiction under Lord Brain was reconvened, and its report was published in 1965. In that year, in addition to the further increase in heroin addiction – with the new cases almost entirely confined to the younger age group – there was also a 'significant increase in the number of addicts who have obtained their drugs entirely from unknown sources'.[6] There was at this stage little evidence of traffic in heroin fed *entirely* from illicit sources, though by 1967 the Home Office had found it impossible to distinguish between addicts who had obtained their drugs from licit sources by illicit means and those who had used illicit sources entirely.

The Brain Report of 1965 pointed out that the major source of supply of heroin had been a small group of doctors who had prescribed very large amounts, and six doctors in London were specifically mentioned. In fact there never was a static group of doctors (the number rarely falling below six or rising above twelve) who prescribed for significant numbers of addicts. The doctors were not the same for any one period, and some of the most appalling instances of irresponsible prescribing occurred after the report had appeared. The 'junkies' doctors' fell into three categories: those who attempted treatment on an outpatient basis, often in liaison with a hospital or nursing home; those who simply maintained the addict with little attempt at 'cure'; and those who exploited and aggravated the situation by massive overprescribing without any real attempt to help. The blanket condemnation of these doctors, often by persons with only a remote contact with addiction, was deplorable. Some of them were dedicated physicians who had for years attempted to help a section of the population whom most of their colleagues would not touch, and they carried out their lonely task without support or help from medical officialdom. Indeed it is possible that had more doctors involved themselves with addicts at an early stage, the development of the British heroin scene would have been very different.

The Brain Report recommended that only licensed doctors should be able to prescribe heroin and cocaine for addicts, and that they should be compelled to notify all such addicts to a central authority. Most of the recommendations of the report were embodied in the Dangerous Drugs Act 1967 and the regulations which followed it. The Dangerous Drugs (Notification of Addicts) Regulations 1968 came into effect on 22 February 1968 and required doctors who attended a person whom they considered or suspected to be an addict to notify the Home Office. The Dangerous Drugs (Supply to Addicts) Regulations 1968 which came into effect on 16 April 1968 prohibited doctors who were not licensed by the Secretary of State from prescribing heroin and cocaine for addicts. At the same time the long-awaited 'treatment centres' began to appear.

Until the late 1960s there was a fairly clear line of demarcation between those young people who took drugs by the oral route (amphetamines and other pills) and those who injected (heroin, cocaine, and opium derivatives). The injectors were a small minority among drug users. The shift towards injectible drug use was clearly evident during the epidemic of Methedrine use in 1968, and it is essential to recognise the crucial historical role of Methedrine in bringing the process of injection closer to the centre of the youth drug cultures.

The spread of the needle culture

As I explained in Chapter Two, the spread of injectible Methedrine in the late 1960s was a major factor in bringing together the pill takers and the injecting users. The drug scene has never been the same since the Methedrine crisis. Today when we consider intravenous drug use we have to take into account the amphetamines and benzodiazepines as much as heroin and cocaine. However, treatment facilities have been more geared to the use of heroin, and there is considerable evidence that cocaine and amphetamine users constitute a major section of those untouched by the medical facilities. As a result, cocaine and amphetamine users are a high-risk group for HIV infection.

Since those years three aspects of change in the use of injectible drugs need to be emphasised. First is the growth of 'poly-drug use' by the intravenous route. During the last two decades there has grown up a 'needle culture' in which many users inject whatever they can get hold of. This pattern of 'poly-drug use' involves heroin, cocaine, amphetamine, sedatives and a range of other substances. Many people believe that the really important distinction is not between the types of substance used, but rather between those who inject and those who do not.

Secondly, there is the spread of illicit heroin throughout Britain. Prior to the late 1960s all the heroin in use in Britain was pure, legal and manufactured to standards laid down in the *British Pharmacopoeia.* The first reliable news report noting the arrival of illegally imported heroin in Britain appeared in *The Times* on 26 March 1969, and its author was Norman Fowler, later to have some responsibility in this area in the government. But powder heroin had begun to appear as early as 1966. Today research and informal observation indicate that heroin is the major drug in use in many areas. According to recent government statistics, 52 per cent of addicts claimed that heroin was their main drug, while a study of drug users in the north-west of England showed a figure of 63 per cent. According to one recent study, one in five people arrested by police in Britain have been using heroin. Moreover, in contrast to the pattern in the 1950s and 1960s, the heroin is virtually all illicit, originating from criminal syndicates located in Turkey, Afghanistan, Pakistan, Iran, Hong Kong and elsewhere. More will be said about the criminal market in Chapter Five.

Thirdly, there is the spread of 'crack' cocaine, referred to in the preceding chapter. 'Crack' is often portrayed as a new drug but it is in fact simply a form of cocaine, free-base cocaine. Cocaine hydrochloride powder is dissolved in water and heated with a chemical reagent to free the cocaine alkaloid base from the salt. Its popularity is related to the swiftness of its action – a 'high' within ten seconds, reaching a peak in a few minutes, and wearing off in around twelve minutes. There was a massive rise in the use of 'crack' cocaine in New York City in 1989–91, and in 1989 there were 53,915 arrests for cocaine in the New York Police Department. On 20 April 1989 Robert Stutman, then senior agent of the New York Division of the Drug Enforcement Administration, addressed the Association of Chief Police Officers in Britain on the danger of 'crack', and predicted a similar increase in Britain. While its use has undoubtedly increased, the epidemic spread which was predicted by Stutman and other observers in the USA has not occurred in Britain on the scale envisaged. At the same time, the use of 'crack' cocaine does present very serious problems in a number of areas, where it is linked with criminal gangs and associated violence. By 1994 hospitals in Leeds, Manchester, Bristol and elsewhere were dealing with increased numbers of babies born to 'crack' users who showed all the symptoms of dependence.

In relation to both heroin and cocaine – along with other street drugs – there is a constant problem of impurity and adulteration. Today heroin is adulterated and of questionable quality although the potency has certainly increased in most places in recent years. Some data suggests that the degree of adulteration has been exaggerated.[7] From the time when most illicit heroin was very impure, there has certainly been an increase in potency in most districts in the last decade. The same is true of cocaine. More will be said about street purity in Chapter Five.

As illicit heroin and cocaine have spread, so the danger of diseases associated with the conditions of use – dirty needles, sharing of equipment, impure material, and so on – has increased. Attention has been focused on HIV and AIDS, but there are also problems with hepatitis B and C. Between 10 and 20 per cent of people with hepatitis C are likely to develop cirrhosis, and some of these will develop liver cancer. There is also the problem of overdose as a result of uncertainty about potency. Recently there have been a number of deaths in north-east Scotland as a result of the spread of what the local police have called 'extremely pure' heroin, that is, four times the normal strength.

The understanding of addiction

> Junk is not, like alcohol or weed, a means to increase enjoyment.
> Junk is not a kick. It is a way of life.
>
> (William Burroughs, 1966)[8]

When heroin is injected intravenously, directly into the bloodstream, it is broken down into morphine and its byproducts, and morphine is accumulated quickly in the lungs, liver and kidneys. After injection the new addict feels an overwhelming sense of peace and drowsy euphoria. One addict recorded her early feelings on heroin.

> Ever flipped out? Gone out beyond the wind? On a crystal yet brutal breeze? So that one blast could break and shatter you, yet give you such joy that you could retreat again and be happy? Once I was happy, high, high on H. A mainline fix would send me way out. But never psychic. I never cared. On hash I got high, everything swam in dark, dark, dizzy waves of sheer heaven. And such bliss. And yet there was something else. Then H. Oh my God, such heaven. Yet at first I was only elated. Pleasure. Then one day more than one jack and I got high, so high. Oh wonderful. I hope I never forget, and that I can remember that heaven. Because it is my life. And possibly my death. But I don't care. If I could die this way I'd be happy.

Physical dependence can quickly follow heroin use, although it needs to be emphasised that both physical and psychological dependence are very variable, and many people do in fact give up the drug at some stage without serious ill-effects. There are many generalisations in this area which are based on individual experience without adequate comparative work. It is perfectly true that many people become dependent on heroin very quickly. But there is nothing automatic about it. Opiates and other intravenously used drugs are not universally attractive. The fear that a very large percentage of any population could be in danger of becoming addicted is almost certainly false. However, the euphoria described above is not long-lasting, and, as the addict becomes more dependent, so he or she needs to increase the dosage in order to experience the previous effect. After a while, the drug is used almost entirely to avoid the terrors of withdrawal.

The presence of an 'abstinence syndrome' or 'withdrawal symptoms' is generally seen as the primary characteristic of physical dependence, and some would argue for its centrality in the understanding of addiction itself. With heroin the mild signs of abstinence include yawning, rhinorrhoea, tears, sweating and anorexia, while moderate symptoms include trembling, goose flesh, abdominal cramps and insomnia, and severe symptoms include restlessness, vomiting, diarrhoea and weight loss. The 'terrrors' of withdrawal play a major role in addict mythology, and fear of 'cold turkey' (coming off the drug without medication) goes very deep. One addict wrote:

> It is almost impossible for someone who isn't and who never has been an addict to know what drugs mean to a junkie. A cure might sound very simple to you – the end of his troubles. But to him it's terrifying – anything he was trying to escape will come back in force. It's like being abandoned on a desert island or being in a crowded room of people whom you don't know – you feel very lost and inadequate. The actual withdrawal also scares him. You can tell him till you're blue in the face that he won't feel anything – or not too much. He won't believe you. (I don't believe people who say it doesn't hurt. The only thing I believe doesn't is narcosis. Do you remember I was frightened of going to X Hospital because they would take me off in 48 hours?) This fear can also be an excuse to stay on. If an addict really wants to come off badly enough he'll go cold turkey. But fear of withdrawal is very real – especially cold turkey, which is why the junkie is often afraid of the police, even if he hasn't done anything. Don't minimise this fear as if you were an irate parent telling your child that there were no snakes in the bed, because he'll just say, 'You don't understand', and he'll be right.

The compulsion to avoid the pain of withdrawal is seen by many, addicts and observers, as being central to the addictive process. The late Alfred Lindesmith, one of the most respected American students of opiate use, argued that addiction is truly present when withdrawal distress comes to be interpreted in relation to the absence of heroin. On this theory, the overwhelming need to avoid the abstinence syndrome is the determining factor.

Whether this is the case or not, it is clear that the addict develops a complex set of responses and conditioning to the drug. Some have argued that the dominant function of the opiates is to gratify primary needs of hunger, fear of pain, and sexual urges. Certainly the relationship of addiction to sexuality is important, and has recurred throughout the literature. One writer commented:

> Over and over again one hears addicts describe the effects of the injection in sexual terms. One addict said that after a fix he felt as if he were coming from every pore. Another said that he used to inject the solution in a rhythmic fashion until it was all used up, and said that this was akin to masturbation, albeit much better.[9]

There are numerous accounts which connect addiction with sexual confusion and turmoil. In the 1960s Isidor Chein and his colleagues noted the degree of sexual confusion among New York addicts, while in a study of female heroin addicts in Holloway Prison in London a few years later, Paul D'Orban observed that 'disturbed psychosexual development was one of the most striking findings'.[10] By comparsion with this degree of disturbance, D'Orban concluded, the heroin addiction seemed a minor symptom. This connects with the classic psychoanalytic view of addiction as the creation of an artificial sexual model rooted in adolescent masturbation. The process of injection replaces intercourse as the focal point of sexual experience. There is undoubtedly support for this 'blood orgasm' thesis in the loss of interest in, and withdrawal from, ordinary sexual relationships which one finds with many addicts.

It is certainly true that many addicts show severe emotional problems, and the recognition of this fact shows that to label them simply as addicts is to isolate the drug use in a highly artificial way, just as it is to assume that those who seek to deal with their emotional problems in some other way are fundamentally different. However, we need to be careful here too. There has been a tradition of relating addiction to a particular type of personality, the so-called 'pre-addictive personality'. But it is not clear that there is such a personality.

The history of addiction shows an enormous variety of personalities, and their social contexts also vary.

We need to take care to avoid simple-minded and one-dimensional views. One very simple-minded view is that the addict seeks 'escape'. Of course, there is a dimension of escape in most forms of drug use, though it is drugs like alcohol and other hypnosedatives which are more suited to those who seek oblivion. Again, the association of addiction with psychopathy was popularised in the USA by Lawrence Kolb, though the British psychiatrists Max Glatt and Jim Willis have also suggested that many addicts were psychopathic personalities.[11] It is quite likely that heroin appeals to the immature and inadequate. Those who cannot establish relationships with people may turn to the drug for security and warmth, though eventually for deliverance from the pain of its absence. Yet at the end of the day this cannot be an adequate account. There are at least enough examples of addicts who do not fit these descriptions to call it into question.

The heroin addict is only too well aware of reality: it is reality itself which has become unmanageable. The issue is not escape but how to cope with an unbearable degree of pain. In the face of a perceived inadequacy, the drug is seen as an instrument of coping. As Lindesmith argued, the purpose of heroin is to make the addict feel normal. The trouble is that all these theories assume that addiction is related only to personal pathology and disturbance. They have tended to ignore external social and economic factors. They may have a validity in their own right, but they are unsatisfactory as total accounts of the situation. We do need to be wary of simplistic accounts of the addictive process, and to be open to the recognition that, just as addiction is a complex phenomenon, so the search for its origins will be multi-dimensional and complex. Just as there are many myths (in the popular sense of falsehoods) about addiction, so it has been suggested that, in the deeper and more accurate understanding of the word, addiction is itself a myth.[12] Yet, whatever the aetiology, once addiction has developed there is a state of psychological imprisonment. The world in which the addict operates is drastically reduced, the territory increasingly limited with predictable events and ritual repetitions.

Treatment for addiction

The understanding of the roots of addiction inevitably affects the approach to treatment. If the addict is seen as a highly disturbed personality, then simply to withdraw drugs will not suffice. The whole area of counselling and psychotherapy in relation to addiction raises complex problems. Some approaches emphasise the physical, perhaps neurological, basis of addiction, and in treatment physical approaches – chemotherapy or even neurosurgical interventions (stereotactic surgery – will be emphasised more than psychological ones. Those who seek a single and straightforward 'solution' will be frustrated, but this is a necessary part of the situation.

Methadone

There is one aspect of treatment which is fairly simple. The management of the physical withdrawal syndrome is relatively straightforward, the normal method being to reduce the amount of heroin and substitute methadone, perhaps first by injection, then in tablet or linctus form. On an outpatient basis, the use of large amounts of methadone acts as a heroin antagonist or blockade, and this has become known as the 'methadone maintenance' programme, based on the early work of Dole and Nyswander in the USA.[13] Other drugs, such as cyclazocine, have also been used, as have various therapies, including aversion therapy and hypnosis. But this is only the beginning. The most important aspect of treatment for addiction is that of the care of the addict in the community, which I will examine further in Chapter Six.

The prescribing of opiates such as heroin remains a controversial area. From the 1920s until 1968 it was common for doctors to prescribe heroin (as well as cocaine and methadone) for addicts. Since the establishment of the clinics, heroin prescribing has declined. However, in recent years, there has been a revival of the practice in some places, and it may well be that this will spread.[14] Whatever happens, heroin will continue to be used and valued in the treatment of terminal pain.

4

Cannabis and the 'Psychedelics'

Cannabis

> More has been written about cannabis than is known about it.
>
> (Dr Max Glatt, 1966)[1]
>
> In time, marijuana on its own leads to incurable insanity.
>
> (Lord Sandford, 1967)[2]
>
> We know next to nothing about the human pharmacology and psychological and social effects of the drug.
>
> (*The Lancet*, 1963)[3]

Cannabis sativa is the name of the hemp plant which grows throughout the world. From the plant is derived not only hemp rope (at one time used for mountaineering, including many Everest expeditions) but also substances which have drug effects, chiefly marijuana (from the flowering leaves and tops) and hashish (the sticky resinous substance).

In spite of attempts to date them earlier, the first reliable references to cannabis probably date from around 500 BC. Later Herodotus described the Scythians of South Russia who threw hemp seed on the fire and inhaled it. It is often said that cannabis is mentioned in the pharmacopoeia of the Chinese Emperor Shen Nung in 2737 BC, but Shen Nung was a mythical figure and his pharmacopoeia cannot be dated much earlier than the ninth century.[4]

The first English reference to cannabis occurs in *Culpepper's Herbal* of 1652. Culpepper regarded it as 'so well known to every good housewife in the country that I shall not need to write any description of it'. There has been considerable use of the plant throughout British history, and it is only recently that its use has been seen as harmful. It was used by Lewis Carroll, John Stuart Mill and William James. In 1956 Stephen Ward, in a lecture to the Women's Adjustment Board, introduced a recipe for hashish fudge, and this curious recipe survives in a well-known paperback cookery book.[5]

In the early twentieth century the drug was brought into the southern states of the USA by Mexican workers, and by 1926 New Orleans was the main centre of its use. It was particularly popular among jazz musicians, and it figures in a variety of jazz tunes under various nicknames such as Muggles (Louis Armstrong, 1928), Chant of Weed (Don Redman, 1931), Sweet Marijuana Brown (Barney Bigard, 1945), and Stoned (Wardle Gray, 1948).

There is no evidence of the smoking (as distinct from chewing or drinking) of cannabis before the sixteenth century, that is, before the practice of smoking, which originated in America, came into contact with cannabis, an old world drug. For many years cannabis was known, misleadingly, as Indian Hemp, and one of its products, hemp rope, was used in mountain climbing. The term Indian Hemp was the main western name of the plant until 1753 when Linnaeus named it *cannabis sativa.* In 1964 India House, upset at the damage to the image of India, asked the Home Office if they would instruct magistrates to stop using this term. One of the Old Street magistrates replied that he had always called it Indian Hemp and had no intention of using the new-fangled name of cannabis.

Cannabis remains the most popular illicit substance used by young people in Britain, as all the surveys indicate. A BBC survey in 1973 claimed that just under four million people in Britain had used cannabis. One recent study suggests that 800 tonnes of cannabis are consumed every year in the UK by around 2.75 million people. According to an Exeter University study of 1995, just under 33 per cent of boys and 27 per cent of girls, aged 15–16, claimed to have used cannabis at some time. In a survey in 1997, 30 per cent of young people aged 14–15 claimed to have used it, while another survey in the same year produced a figure of 35 per cent of 15-year-olds. According to the Trimbos Institute in Utrecht, more young people in the UK use cannabis than in any other country in Europe (including the Netherlands).

Much of the enforcement activity involves cannabis. At least 85 per cent of all drugs seizures relate to cannabis. In 1995, according to the House of Commons library records, there were 91,325 seizures of cannabis in contrast to 6468 of heroin.

Strictly speaking, cannabis is not a drug but a plant which produces drug effects under certain circumstances. Botanically the cannabis plant stands between the hop and the stinging nettle, and its centrally acting, intoxicant and relaxing qualities have made it a popular intoxicant for hundreds of years, as well as a sacramental aid in some religious traditions. The potency of cannabis as a drug depends mostly on the presence of the main active principle, delta-9 trans-tetrahydrocannabinol (THC). The THC content of some plants may be very slight, though the resin (hashish) contains more of the active principle than the flowering leaves (marijuana). Pure THC can be very powerful and can trigger a psychotic episode, though the idea of a specific 'cannabis psychosis' is discredited by most commentators.

The cannabis which circulates in Britain varies considerably in potency, and strong varieties are always sought out eagerly by those in the know. In the last few years 'Skunk' and 'Northern Lights' have been very popular, selling at around £240 per ounce in 1994. A study of confiscated cannabis in 1973 showed that the difference between the strongest and the weakest sample was 30,000 per cent.

While a distinguished psychiatrist commented in 1966 that 'more has been written about cannabis than is known about it', this is no longer accurate. The scientific literature is clearer in its assessment of the effects of the cannabis plant than is the case with many other botanical substances, and the conclusions of detailed studies are overwhelmingly uniform. There are still many claims which are not clear (such as the possibility of chromosomal damage, or the effects of the build-up in body fat) and there is much still to be learned (which is hampered by legal constraints on research), but there is a remarkable consistency in the international data. While positions on the control of cannabis vary, the general consensus on its effects – (from the older reports such as those of the Indian Hemp Drugs Commission (1854) and the Mayor of New York's Committee on Marijuana (1944) down to the Wootton Committee in Britain (1968) – is that this is a fairly mild intoxicant, and that, in the words of the Wootton Committee, 'the long term consumption of cannabis in moderate doses has no harmful effects'. Even the National Commission on Marihuana and Drug Abuse, set up by President Nixon and filled with conservatives, concluded that the drug was relatively harmless.[6] The medical journal *The Lancet*, in an editorial in 1995, claimed that the smoking of cannabis, even long-term, is not harmful to health, while two researchers from Harvard Medical School in 1997 described it as 'possibly the safest therapeutically active substance known to humanity'. Fatalities are virtually unknown. An Australian study in 1988 reported that 'a search of the literature did not find any reports of death from acute toxicity from cannabis'.[7]

Of course, like any substance, cannabis is open to abuse. But most cannabis use is episodic, rather than heavy or chronic. Those who are permanently intoxicated are a very small minority indeed, and it is among this small group that some observers have identified what is termed an 'amotivational syndrome', a cumulative lethargy in which all motivation disappears and energy is sapped.[8] It is emphatically not the general pattern among users. Indeed it has been claimed that cannabis is unique among drugs in that, whereas the pattern of most illicit drug use is that people either stop using a drug or increase the dosage, the pattern with cannabis seems to be that, while there are more regular users than occasional, there seems to be no general trend towards increasing the amount used. Most cannabis use is recreational and is not at all related to an addictive or destructive lifestyle. Nevertheless, cannabis has been subject to more irrational attacks than any other substance in the last few decades.

There are three questions which regularly arise in relation to cannabis: those of 'escalation', of 'cannabis psychosis', and of the medical use of the drug. The first relates to the question of progression from cannabis to other, more harmful drugs, and it is often referred to as 'escalation', though this is a military term, and those who use it often tend to read the conclusion into the premise. It is worth examining each of these questions briefly.

Cannabis and escalation

> The increase in heroin addiction in young people follows exactly the same curve as that of the increase in the number of cannabis convictions.
>
> (Dr Elizabeth Tylden, 1969)[9]
>
> Close parallelism between curves can be notoriously non-informative.
>
> (Professor C. R. B. Joyce, 1969)[10]

The escalation thesis in its more simplistic form claims that young people 'start' on cannabis and 'escalate' to drugs such as heroin. In this form it is still frequently heard from people who are, on other subjects, quite rational and logical in their thinking. No serious commentators would accept it in this crude version, for it is demonstrably clear that most cannabis users do not progress in this way. On a world scale there are many places where cannabis is common and heroin unknown, others where heroin addiction is a serious problem but where cannabis does not figure.

In Britain too, it is clear that the escalation thesis is a serious misreading of the evidence. Indeed, Plant and others have argued that in many cases there is a 'de-escalation' process in which cannabis remains the main drug of choice. Users often try other drugs but then revert to cannabis, and its use itself tends to be reduced.[11] Where progression does take place, it is generally agreed that this is due to social and economic factors, and not to anything inherent in the drug. Many have argued that, as a result of the criminalisation of cannabis, users may be led into criminal cultures, including those which form in prison, and as a result are drawn to other drugs and other forms of criminal activity. The realisation that one of the main dangers of cannabis is that of arrest, leading to association with more serious forms of crime, has led police in many areas to treat the crime of cannabis possession as equivalent to a traffic offence.

The escalation thesis is still put forward, usually without any evidence, often by means of faulty conclusions drawn from incorrect data. Thus it is often argued that the rise in use of cannabis coincided historically with the increase in notifications of heroin addicts. Within certain places and during specific periods of time, this is quite true, but the argument falls into an elementary statistical trap of confusing correlative and causal connections. The fact that two movements or trends occur during the same period does not indicate that they are causally related. If, for example, over a fifty-year period in Britain, the number of storks declined at the same time that the number of children born also declined, this could lead people to the erroneous conclusion that children were delivered by storks. After 1945 there was a close correlation between the per capita consumption of bananas, the issue of radio licences by the Post Office, and the admission rates to psychiatric hospitals.

For the argument that cannabis use leads to addiction to drugs such as heroin to stand up would require evidence of a causal connection between the two, and the evidence not only does not support such a view but flatly contradicts it. Moreover, there is abundant evidence of hundreds of thousands of cannabis users who do not make this progression. The escalation thesis does not stand up to serious analysis.

Cannabis and psychosis

> Chronic intake causes a characteristic chronic psychosis.
> (Dr Elizabeth Tylden, 1968)[12]
>
> Cannabis does not produce psychoses.
> (Dr O. Moraes Andrade, 1964)[13]

The rhetoric about any drug-induced psychosis is almost always a mixture of pharmacology, race, culture, ignorance, myth and history. We need to recognise the danger of projecting a simple causal link between any drug and any form of mental illness. Psychosis itself is a slippery concept, and in recent years approaches to it have fallen into two main areas, the biochemical and the socio-cultural. The debates have been both about aetiology and about interpretation. The concept of psychosis is not a neutral one. The existence of perceptual change may be seen as a fact; the labelling of such change as psychotic (or mystical or ego-transcending or whatever) is a matter of opinion. This is a factor which recurs throughout the study of drug cultures as well as that of mental health and sickness.

The idea of a specific cannabis psychosis dates from 1843. Since then there have been innumerable articles about it, yet cannabis psychosis remains a questionable concept and the descriptions of it in the literature are often very unsophisticated. The Indian Hemp Drugs Commission in 1894 questioned such a concept, while in the USA there were few references to it after the 1920s. The toxicologist David E. Smith of the Haight-Ashbury Free Clinic in San Francisco claimed in 1968 that out of 35,000 patients seen at the clinic throughout the peak period of the 'hippie' culture when cannabis use was endemic, he had encountered no cases of cannabis psychosis. Sir Aubrey Lewis' survey of the clinical data in his appendix to the Wootton Report noted that the accounts of the syndrome 'include practically every known variety of mental disorder', and that there was no clear evidence for a specific psychotic condition with a causal link to cannabis. The appendix cast doubt on the existence of such a syndrome as did the Canadian government's report of 1970. A recent American paper studied 9434 cases in the Boston area and concluded that there were no convincing cases. There are many reports from India, Morocco, Nigeria, the Gambia, and elsewhere. A recent study from the Gambia raised the key question: does cannnabis or any other drug initiate a psychosis or simply unmask it? Many of the recent reports of cannabis psychosis come from Morocco where between 1958 and 1965 there were 600 cases of acute psychosis in an area of high cannabis consumption.

That there may be a link between drug use and psychosis is not seriously disputed. The key issue is that of whether there is a causal link. Heather Ashton has pointed out that the mechanisms of the brain are no more fully understood than are those of cannabis, and that any drug can trigger a 'psychotic episode'. As I have pointed out above, the establishing of simplistic causal connections and judgements based on statistical correlations is a well-known minefield.

Recent studies in Britain on racial and ethnic factors in diagnosis have suggested that Caribbean males (who are not the majority of cannabis users in the UK) seem to be disproportionately represented among those categorised in this way. Littlewood and Lipsedge have claimed that most of those diagnosed as suffering from cannabis psychosis are wrongly diagnosed. They and others have stressed that, while most cannabis users in the UK are white, almost all the cases of cannabis psychosis involve black people. Writers in the *British Journal of Psychiatry* in 1987 claimed that cannabis psychosis seemed to be a uniquely West Indian diagnosis. According to one study, covering 1984–86, black men aged between 16 and 44 were 12–13 times more likely than others to be diagnosed as schizophrenic, while in other studies the figure is as high as 29 times more. The question of whether cannabis psychosis is a racist diagnosis, and the extent to which race and culture affects diagnosis of psychoses in general, is a major area of concern.

Of course, cannabis, like most centrally acting substances, can trigger a psychotic episode in a predisposed individual. But who is 'prone to psychosis'? Would they have become psychotic anyway, drug or no drug? The whole field of predisposition is very tricky. It is certainly true that many addicts of heroin had previously used cannabis. But did one drug predispose them to the other? Are there some people for whom cannabis is highly dangerous while for most people it is not? There has been talk for years about a 'pre-addictive personality'. The problem is that nobody knows with any precision who is predisposed to what. Some years ago officials at the chemical weapons research station at Porton Down assured visitors that they never tested any psychoactive drugs on people who were prone to subsequent mental disorder. When asked what kind of tests were used to discern *subsequent* mental disorder, they said it was an official secret.

While few would disagree that cannabis, like other psychoactive substances, can trigger a psychotic episode in some individuals, it seems, as a mild intoxicant, one of the least likely drugs to do so, and the evidence that it does is slight. The specific 'cannabis psychosis' in particular remains a doubtful entity.[14]

Medical uses of cannabis

There is, finally, the question of the medical use of cannabis, a question which is becoming important again. It was added to the list of proscribed substances in 1925. Tincture of cannabis was prescribed for a range of conditions in the past, but legal prescribing ended in 1971, and was made impossible by the classification of cannabis under Schedule 1 of the Misuse of Drugs Regulations 1985.

It has long been known that cannabis has therapeutic value, and recently there have been new calls for medical availability. A recent study at Harvard showed that half of 1035 oncologists would prescribe it if they were able to do so. It is well known to be of use in treating nausea after chemotherapy and glaucoma, and in helping AIDS patients increase their appetite. Many physicians believe that cannabis can be useful in treatment of multiple sclerosis, rheumatoid arthritis, and chronic back pain, and in the care of cancer patients under chemotherapy.

Already, without much publicity, controls have been relaxed on one active ingredient of cannabis, dronabinol, and the drug Nabilone, originally marketed as Cesamet by Eli Lilly, is now available to people with cancer, multiple sclerosis and other conditions. It has been placed under similar procedures to heroin and cocaine, and we can expect other developments, although it may be some years before the cannabinoids as a whole will be available on prescription.

The debate on decriminalisation and legalisation

Although the two terms are often used interchangeably, strictly speaking decriminalisation means taking a drug out of the effective operation of the criminal law, while legalisation means making it available, with or without restrictions. The calls for decriminalisation of cannabis possession, which have been the subject of debate in the UK for over thirty years, are likely to become more frequent in the coming years. Many police officers support decriminalisation of cannabis though they often feel able to say so only after retirement. Thus the former Assistant Chief Constable of Merseyside, Alison Halford, has argued for decriminalisation, and it is well known that many senior police officers support such a view even if they feel that they cannot say so publicly.[15] Moreover, the recommendations of the Wootton Report of 1968 have largely been incorporated into legal practice. The report opposed imprisonment for cannabis possession, and in 1973 the Lord Chancellor urged magistrates to exercise 'becoming moderation'. The Criminal

Justice Act of 1976 reduced the maximum penalty for possession to three months. Today most cases of cannabis possession are dealt with by a caution.

On 28 September 1997, *The Independent on Sunday* became the first national newspaper to back the demand for legalisation. There is little evidence that church groups are any more involved in this debate than they were thirty years ago, and there has been no significant contribution to the debate from any church source.[16] Nor is there any evidence that the government is willing even to open up the discussion. As Ann Taylor, Chair of the Ministerial Sub-Committee on Drugs, said recently, 'It is just not on our agenda'.[17]

In some respects today the situation is the reverse of that suggested by Max Glatt thirty years ago: today we know more about cannabis, yet the official rhetoric remains the same. The very mild suggestion in 1997 by Clare Short that decriminalisation might be considered – hardly the most radical of suggestions! – was clearly seen as beyond the pale by New Labour. The present position is not helpful to informed debate, and we could be entering another period of regression in terms of serious thought within the government. Indeed, so far as cannabis is concerned, the relationship between the known data and official attitudes is an inverse relationship.

LSD and the 'psychedelic' drugs

> Whenever in doubt, turn off your mind, relax, float downstream.
>
> (Leary, Metzner and Alpert, 1965)[18]
>
> Turn off your mind, relax, and float downstream. This is not dying.
>
> (The Beatles, *Revolver*)
>
> Psychedelic drugs are very much out of fashion. Illicit drugs users have less interest in them now than at any time in the last fifteen years.
>
> (Lester Grinspoon and James Bakalar, 1981)[19]

The word 'psychedelic' (or 'psychodelic' in its initial form) was coined by a British physician, Humphrey Osmond, in 1957. He defined it in this way:

> A psychedelic compound is one like LSD or mescaline which enriches the mind and enlarges the vision. It is this kind of experience which provides the greatest possibility for examining those areas most interesting to psychiatry and which has provided men down the ages with experiences they have considered valuable above all others.[20]

It was not until the 1960s that the word became popular. In its more recent usage the word still refers to substances which enrich the mind and enhance the vision, and it is used about music and arts as well as drugs. In earlier periods, writers such as William James, who experimented with nitrous oxide, and Aldous Huxley, whose work with mescaline led him to speak of 'chemical conditions of transcendental experience', had linked this range of drugs with the quest for higher levels of consciousness. During the same years there had been work on the possibility of a chemical basis for psychosis. However, the existence of 'psychedelic' drugs, as defined above, has been known for centuries. The peyote cactus (*Lophophora williamsii*) was used in Mexican religion as a sacred element, and during the nineteenth century native American tribes reintroduced peyote to the United States from northern Mexico.

The best-known of the psychedelic drugs is lysergic acid diethylamide (LSD-25). Derived from ergot and first discovered by Albert Hoffmann in 1938, LSD is the diethylamide derivative of lysergic acid. It became known to the general population in Britain in 1966, and was central to the growth of the counter-culture which spread from San Francisco to Britain at that time.

However, LSD had been around for some time, and was introduced, not by hippies in the 1960s, but by a small number of psychiatrists with Jungian backgrounds at Powick Hospital in Worcester, in 1951. Its main use was to enable patients to recall early childhood experiences. About seven hundred patients are believed to have been given LSD at Powick. A little later, many people, including Anglican clergy under the supervision of the late Dr Frank Lake, founder of the school of 'clinical theology', were given LSD in therapy. Indeed, it is highly likely that Anglican clergy were among the earliest groups to experience LSD 'trips' under medical supervision.[21]

The use of LSD in treatment of alcoholism was also common – Cary Grant, for instance, was treated with the drug for alcohol problems. However, it was the explosion of the Haight-Ashbury youth counter-culture in 1966 which brought LSD into the mass world of youth drug consumption.

Unlike the stimulants which increase motor activity, and the sedatives which reduce it, the drugs described as 'psychedelic' change the nature and processing of experience. They precipitate a kind of depth charge into the unconscious, which is why they were used in therapy in the first place. The effects of these drugs can be summarised under three heads.

First, they bring about an intensification of visual perception and sensory experience, producing a kaleidoscope of intense light and colour. (They are often misleadingly called 'hallucinogenic' though visual hallucinations may not occur.) Timothy Leary's instructions to psychedelic initiates included this passage.

> You are now witnessing the magical dance of forms.
> Ecstatic kaleidoscopic patterns explode all round you.
> All possible shapes come to life before your eyes,
> The retinal circus,
> The ceasless play of elements –
> Earth, water, air, fire –
> In ever changing forms and manifestations,
> Dazzles you with its complexity and variety.[22]

Secondly, they can bring about an experience of depersonalisation, of ego-loss, and of the symbolic disintegration of the 'real world'. Thus many people under psychedelic drugs experience what they describe as 'ego-transcendence'. The late R. D. Laing called such experiences 'meta-egoic' experiences.

Thirdly, the drugs may illuminate, or distort, reality, so that situations and phenomena come to be viewed differently. Whether one describes such changes as psychosis (with Sidney Cohen and Donald Louria) or mystical insight (with Alan Watts and Timothy Leary) depends on one's perspective. Thus Leary made this claim:

> A psychedelic experience is a journey to new realms of consciousness. The scope and content of the experience is limitless, but its characteristic features are the transcendence of verbal concepts, of space-time dimensions, and of the ego

or identity. Such experiences of enlarged consciousness can occur in a variety of ways: sensory deprivation, yoga exercises, disciplined meditation, religious or aesthetic ecstasies, or spontaneously. Most recently they have become available to anyone through the ingestion of psychedelic drugs such as LSD, psilocybin, mescaline, DMT, etc.[23]

The mass spread of LSD and similar drugs was linked to the concern with expansion of consciousness, and to a profound disenchantment with the conceptual framework of conventional western society. Herbert Marcuse wrote:

> Today's rebels want to see, hear, feel new things in a new way: they link liberation with the dissolution of ordinary and orderly perception. The 'trip' involves the dissolution of the ego shaped by the established society – an artificial and short-lived dissolution . . . Awareness of the need for such a revolution in perception, for a new sensorium, is perhaps the kernel of truth in the psychedelic search.[24]

Many of the claims made for this range of drugs need careful scrutiny. It is not at all clear, for example, that the drug does enhance achievement, though it may enhance the feeling of achievement. Many paintings and drawings done under LSD show a loss of basic skills, and a reduction of complexity and sophistication. But Marcuse's comment about the 'kernel of truth' has abiding significance. It is certainly true that many lives were changed by LSD, and that many individuals, after taking the drug, found that their minds were opened up to new ways of thinking and feeling.

Many, however, had experiences of great terror and disintegration, and some have never fully recovered. The 'adverse reactions' to LSD became known in the late 1960s as 'bad trips'. They became far less common as the drug culture became acclimatised to LSD usage, as the drug and its range of effects became more familiar, and as people learned how to cope with its adverse effects without the help of psychiatrists. Out of the experience of the bad trip came the idea of a calm centre, first set up at Haight-Ashbury Free Medical Clinic. Here, with the help of soft lighting, gentle music, and an atmosphere of calm and security, individuals were 'brought down' and reassured that they were still themselves. The calm centre approach has proved more effective than the crude pharmacological intervention, involving large doses of chlorpromazine, which sadly one still finds occurring. Hence the late Dr Nicholas Malleson's wise warning when, asked what was the worst thing that could happen to a person on a bad LSD trip, he replied that the worst thing was that s/he should fall into the hands of an unsophisticated psychiatrist. As newer drugs circulate, the headline in a 1991 issue of *Druglink* will prove to be true: 'Sixties skills may be needed to cope with a new generation of trippers'.[25]

Associated with LSD have been substances such as STP, PCP, DMT, and derivatives of the psilocybin mushroom. PCP (phencyclidine hydrochlorode), originally known as 'angel dust', has become known by such names as 'super grass' or 'peace weed'.[26]

Since its appearance on the street drug scene in 1966, LSD has declined and risen at various points. A national survey by the Office of Population Censuses and Surveys in 1969 concluded that less than 1 per cent of the population of England and Wales had used LSD. By 1993 there was an increase in use of LSD in a variety of places after a trafficking ring had been arrested in Scarborough in 1992. While historically associated with the growth of a counter-culture, today there is no single cultural or subcultural group associated with the use of this range of drugs. LSD in particular has continued to be a popular drug among young people, many of whom use it more as a stimulant rather than a psychedelic. In spite of much sensational publicity in the late 1960s, the incidence of serious casualties associated with this range of drugs is probably quite small. The history of LSD is one of decline and fall, and it tends to return to popularity from time to time.

Part Three

The Challenge to Pastoral Care

5

The Social Context of Drug Use

> As drug use becomes more widespread, then in a sense it becomes more normal. As the numbers increase, the numbers of those presenting with traditional problems of dependence decline as a percentage in favour of those using drugs as a response to social and environmental rather than personal needs.
>
> (Les Kay and Chris Rowarth, 1985)[1]
>
> I refuse to accept that drugs have become part of growing up.
>
> (George Howarth, MP, 1997)[2]

The social structure of the drug scene: the early years

As research into drug use has increased at almost the same rate as the use of the drugs themselves, the problem of keeping up to date with it has become more acute. Of course, as in other fields, much of the research lacks thoroughness and methodological sophistication, and much of it should be treated with caution. However, a major factor has been that drug use has become more ordinary, drug users more like anyone else, and so at times one suspects that anything that anyone says about patterns of drug use is likely to be true – somewhere. This chapter therefore can only attempt to identify some of the social factors and trends in recent drug use.

It is important to locate drug use within its social context, for all drug effects occur within the framework of interaction between substance, personality and social context. The social structure of drug use among young people is immensely complex, and detailed studies in a variety of areas have shown the danger of stereotypes and the risks of over-simplified accounts. Nevertheless certain general trends and shifts in recent years can be identified and summarised.

In my earlier study of 1970 I examined the historical shifts associated with cannabis use, the growth of an adolescent pill culture, and the different groups of drug users in London and other cities.[3] In that book I looked at three areas in particular: the historical material on cannabis use; the role of the West End of London in the early pill scene; and the various groups of drug takers in Britain's cities. I examined the changing place of cannabis in our society from the 1950s onwards. I looked at the role of London's Soho district in the emergence of the pill scene; and I described the structure of the drug scene as it was at the end of the 1960s. In that survey I looked at six different groups – students, beats, young drifters and homeless people, pillheads, junkies, and hippies. Readers are referred to the earlier study, and to other earlier works, for more detailed treatment, but it is worth mentioning three features of that early history.

First, there was a time, until the early 1960s, when cannabis use was restricted to a number of groups, often referred to as 'subcultures'. These included the early beatniks, the followers of Kerouac, Ferlinghetti and Ginsberg, jazz musicians, some immigrants from Africa and the Caribbean who had come to live in ports and dockland districts such as Cable Street in East London, Tiger Bay in Cardiff, and Liverpool 8, and some of the young people involved with the Campaign for Nuclear Disarmament and the emerging world of contemporary folk music. In 1932 the Home Office reported that 'the illicit use and traffic in the drug appears to be confined to two negro groups in London'. As late as 1966 the criminologist David Downes could claim that there was more likelihood of an Oxford undergraduate or a member of a jazz club coming into contact with drugs than there was of a young delinquent in Stepney or Poplar. Certainly in these years contact with heroin addiction, not only among young people but among young drug takers, was minimal.[4]

Secondly, it is important to note the crucial role of the Soho club culture of the early 1960s in providing a social base for the emerging pill scene among young people. In these years the creation of the big discotheques, the growth of rock music, the rise of Carnaby Street and the Mod culture, and the spread of amphetamines were historically coincident. Soho provided the context and was the distribution point for the pill traffic, and provided the model for other cities to follow.[5]

Thirdly, drugs and homelessness were already linked to some degree in these early years. Although most older homeless people, the habitués of 'Skid Row', were heavily dependent on alcohol (usually cheap wine and cider and methylated spirits), by around 1965 those who were working with 'young drifters' in London were seeing an increase in cannabis and amphetamine (and, a few years later, barbiturate) use among this group. The records of early detached youth work projects such as the Soho, Blenheim and Portobello Projects, and the Salvation Army Rink Project, show this increase clearly.[6]

The hippie scene of the late 1960s

> The interests of our college age and adolescent young in the psychology of alienation, oriental mysticism, psychedelic drugs, and communitarian experiments comprise a cultural constellation that radically diverges from values and assumptions that have been in the mainstream of our society at least since the scientific revolution of the seventeenth century.
>
> (Theodore Roszak, 1969)[7]
>
> Life in Burslem, Tadcaster and Crewe was not greatly affected.
>
> (Laurie Taylor, 1973)[8]

A fourth feature was the hippie scene of the late 1960s which brought about a major transformation in the youth culture of the world. The idea of 'hippie' developed in Haight-Ashbury district of San Francisco, the word itself deriving from a shop called Haight Independent Proprietors. The world's first Psychedelic Shop was opened in Haight Street on 1 January 1966. Yet a year and a half later, on 7 June 1967, the community celebrated 'The Death of Hippie'. A coffin was carried through the district while 'Sergeant Pepper's Lonely Hearts Club Band' was played continuously.

Out of the Haight-Ashbury district came the San Francisco sound, acid rock, with groups such as Jefferson Airplane and the Grateful Dead, the mass spread of cannabis and LSD, and, more significantly, the spread of a counter-culture which has changed, to some degree, the lifestyles and thought-forms of all of us. The seriousness and long-term character of this counter-cultural shift was already recognised by Theodore Roszak in 1969.[9] Roszak spoke of an entire culture of disaffiliation, and, while the influence of the counter-culture on young people was often exaggerated, its long-term signficance is of crucial importance in understanding both the state of drug use and the state of the contemporary world.

Within a short time, however, Haight-Ashbury had been transformed from a gentle community of flower children into a violent and dangerous zone. From the drug perspective, it was the spread of amphetamine which transformed that community as it did so many in Britain. Many hippies retreated to the communes in California and elsewhere, and moved away from compulsive drug use. Indeed David Smith reported in 1970 that the total consumption of drugs in the communes was substantially less than the average American norm.[10] On the other hand, the drug scene itself became more dangerous and more entrenched in this period. A number of commentators in Britain were pointing to the likely growth of more serious drug problems, particularly if the warning signals were ignored, and if Britain followed American approaches. For the most part, these warnings were ignored, with the result that we have reaped the whirlwind.[11]

Some recent changes

Since those days a number of major changes have occurred. The first has been the spread of drug use down the socio-economic scale. Until the mid-1960s most use of heroin and cocaine, and indeed most forms of drug addiction, occurred among middle-class people, with a strong sprinkling of the aristocracy. Although David Downes, in his 1966 study, claimed that drug use played a minimal role in urban working-class delinquent life, he added that this did not imply that the 'drug cult' would not 'spread down the socio-economic scale'.[12] In fact, such a spread occurred within a few years of his words. By the late 1960s there was a significant number of working-class addicts.

Most of the early amphetamine users probably came from working-class backgrounds. What has been striking about the developments since the early 1980s has been the spread of heroin and cocaine use to a much wider section of young people. The pattern in Britain has in many ways been the reverse of that in the USA. While in the USA the use of injectible drugs, heroin in particular, began in the ghetto districts and spread, around 1970, to the middle class, the British pattern was one of middle-class use, moving into working-class communities later.

The second change has been the growth of a rave culture. The spread of 'recreational' drugs has changed the face of the British drug scene. Of course, drugs have been used recreationally for thousands of years. However, the mass consumption of drugs other than alcohol in a recreational setting is relatively new in Britain. Taking its origins from the house music culture, which spread from Chicago to Britain, rave has, through a combination of music, technology and chemicals, created a whole 'night-time economy'.

What is the appeal of rave? It has been seen by some commentators as the closest many young people today get to something akin to religious ecstasy. For many thousands of young people, 'rave' is a way of letting go: it provides an experience of being part of a mass movement of closeness and happiness, friendship, warmth and excitement, and a temporary release from the monotony and dreariness of daily life. There has in recent years been a massive growth of all-night rave clubs in the Greater London area. Here 'ecstasy' tablets have been selling at around £15 per tablet, and every weekend about £7.5 million worth of drugs are sold. By 1996 the price of a tablet was down to £5 in some places, partly as a result of the appearance of high-quality material from Holland. There has been a general price fall in the last ten years from £20 to £5. In Britain, the rave capital of the world, it is estimated that around 1.5 million ecstasy or ecstasy-related tablets are taken each week by around a million young people.

As I explained in Chapter Two, almost all the use of ecstasy in Britain is club-based. So are most of the associated problems as young people have been caught up in the commercial conflicts between pubs and clubs. Clubs used by ravers have needed to make a profit, and an obvious way to do so has been by the sale of bottled water. So club officials would turn up the heating and switch off the cold water taps. Most of the deaths have been the result of dehydration, and of the desperate need for fresh cold water, or of an allergic reaction to the drugs. However, too much cold water can dilute the salts and sugars in the body, and flood the kidneys. Since the early tragedies, many clubs have established 'chill-out' rooms which provide slower music and have a cooler temperature.[13]

> I feel very pessimistic. Until recently the UK was a drug backwater. I used to think that it would continue to be so while we had low unemployment. Now that there is no indication that unemployment is falling, there is little hope of solving the drug problem.
>
> (Dr Martin Plant, 1984)[14]

A third change has been the increased association of drug use with high unemployment, social deprivation and homelessness. Until the late 1960s, the absence of 'addict neighbourhoods' of the New York City type was one of the clearest features of the British heroin scene (which, in fact, meant the London scene). Today, by contrast, heroin use in particular is far more highly correlated with economic deprivation and unemployment than was the case in the earlier period. The reasons for this are complex, and are partly because of the financial appeal of the heroin market as an alternative economy, partly because of the targeting of certain deprived districts by heroin dealers, and partly because of the historic appeal of heroin, with its powerful analgesic qualities, to those experiencing profound hopelessness and despair about the future. This needs to be understood carefully. It is certainly not correct to claim, as some do, that the most serious problems of illicit drug use are now associated only with deprived communities or with high unemployment. Nor is it true to say that the 'ghetto' pattern, associated for so long with American cities, has been reproduced in the UK. But there is some truth in both these statements. While unemployment and youth alienation are not the only factors in the situation, there is certainly a far closer link between heroin use and high unemployment than was the case before the 1980s. Probably 80 per cent of addicts in Scotland, for example, are unemployed or in prison.

The link between drug traffic and unemployment and economic collapse can be seen in many towns. If we look, for example, at Grimethorpe, part of Barnsley in South Yorkshire, we see a pattern which is repeated elsewhere. This is a community which had been utterly dependent on its mine. Today, as the pit lies derelict and unused, and as unemployment stands at 95 per cent in some districts, the devastation is horrifying, with whole rows of houses vandalised, burnt out or abandoned. The sense of being a community without future is palpable. It is hardly surprising that there was a 300 per cent increase in heroin use in Barnsley between 1992 and 1995. One driver was arrested with £11 million worth of heroin. But Grimethorpe does not stand alone, and it is likely that we will see more and more British towns which manifest the same conditions. Take the Lancashire town of Bolton where, according to one of its Members of Parliament, drug traffic takes place in districts where the streets have been 'turned into barren places'.[15]

A related factor is the increased link between drugs and prostitution. The East End of London has been a centre for young prostitutes, or, to use the term they prefer, sex workers, since the 1940s. Recently there has been a significant increase in the numbers of sex workers who are also rough sleepers and who use heroin and crack cocaine. The Marigold Project, part of the Young Women's Christian Association (YWCA), has been working with these women for some time. Between January and May 1997 the workers were in contact with 87, of whom 75 per cent were using heroin and 65 per cent crack cocaine. Only 24 per cent were in touch with local drugs services, and only 41 per cent had knowledge of them. In a period of eighteen weeks the workers distributed 7992 condoms, but this practical concern with a group which is highly vulnerable to HIV and AIDS is only one aspect of a deeper concern for the women as people.

The following three cases are fairly typical of the sex workers in the East End.

> Irene is 15, of mixed race, and uses crack cocaine. She absconded from council care, having been placed there as a result of sexual abuse at home. She has not felt able to

attend drugs agencies. She has no pimp, and has been raped and assaulted on a number of occasions.

Barbara also uses crack cocaine. She is a self-mutilator. She has experienced rape, robbery, verbal abuse, and physical assault. She has a teenage son who is also a crack user. She wants to stop her drug use and has received some help from local agencies.

Theresa is 25 and has three children. She has been 'on the game' for seven years to support her children. She uses alcohol when working. She has an unemployed boyfriend who is addicted to alcohol and gambling. She often works on the streets only in order to pay the gas and electricity bills. She has been violently raped, and the only one of the Marigold workers whom she would trust with her story was a priest.

The experience of the Marigold Project workers corresponds with that of other agencies in a number of respects. The young drug users who have become sex workers have often done so simply to support their habit or for related economic reasons. (Cuts in child benefits to single parents, as suggested recently, will almost certainly increase the numbers involved in prostitution.) These young women are often ignorant to an alarming degree both about drugs and drugs facilities, and about sex. Many of them have virtually no knowledge of medical or social facilities, local drugs projects, and so on.[16]

There is also evidence from a number of parts of the country to indicate that the use of drugs other than alcohol, the traditional drug of 'Skid Row', is now common among homeless people. In North American cities, the spread of 'crack' cocaine has been identified as one of the key elements in the changing pattern of homelessness. While there is no evidence of an inevitable causal link either way round (i.e. drugs cause homelessness, or homelessness leads to drug use), data from both the USA and Britain does suggest that crack cocaine has significantly affected the street homeless scene. While alcohol remains the favoured drug among homeless people, many young homeless have become so through their crack use, while others have found the drug an aid to survival.[17] Caution must be exercised here, and the patterns of drug use among homeless people are immensely varied. Nevertheless the fact that more homeless people now use drugs such as cocaine, and the fact that more people become homeless as a result of their drug use, are both important factors in the changing scene.

Again, while there are no precise parallels to the ghettoes of North America, London and other British cities and towns now possess areas in which high drug use is part of an economy controlled by criminal syndicates (see below). Ralph Tefferteller worked for many years at the Henry Street Settlement in the Lower East Side of New York City. Here the addicts grew up in crowded lower-class neighbourhoods and were introduced to heroin at the age of 11. When Tefferteller's book *The Addict in the Street*[18] was published in Britain, it was the sharp contrast with the British scene which reviewers noticed. Today it would be the parallels. Tefferteller's book tells a story which is common in the ghetto districts of virtually all American cities, and in recent years the pattern has become true for British cities too. Again we need to exercise very great caution in making too close parallels, and there remain many differences and contrasts between the two countries, not least in their approaches to drug treatment.

> None of the prohibited drugs are a serious risk to health: the risks come about entirely from the dirty, secret, criminal circumstances in which, under prohibition, drugs of unknown strength and composition are consumed.
>
> (Dr John Marks, 1997)[19]

Fourthly, there is the increased role of the criminal syndicates. The involvement of criminal syndicates in the circulation of illicitly manufactured drugs goes back to the years of prohibition of alcohol in the USA. It is from these years that Mafia control dates. In relation to Britain, the original syndicates involved were the Hong Kong Triads whose role in the distribution of 'Chinese' heroin goes back to the early days of the Dangerous Drugs Act 1967. The Triads are still active and growing. Since then, however, the scene has shifted with groups from Iran, Afghanistan, Pakistan and, most recently and significantly, Turkey playing the lead, while the South Americans dominate the cocaine trade. Groups from Jamaica also figure in the cocaine traffic, and some potent amphetamine has come from criminal groups in Poland. Recently also there has been an increase in the production of heroin in Colombia. Within Britain, involvement with the traffic involves a wide range of individuals, some of whom have roots in older criminal groups. For example, some well-known London criminals with a history of activity in the area of pornography have recently reappeared in connection with amphetamine traffic via Ireland. Most terrorism in the world is funded from drug traffic which ranks second to arms traffic in the field of syndicated crime.[20]

A major change in the street drug scene, which is to a large extent a result of the criminalising of the traffic, has been the close link which is now obvious between certain drugs and violence. This link is most evident in, though not restricted to, certain parts of large cities. Dublin, for instance, has witnessed an increase in drug-related gangland assassinations. During 1996–7 there was an average of one murder per month there which was believed to be related to a drug syndicate. More generally, it has been claimed that around 50 per cent of all crimes of property and theft are drug-related. In 1995 heroin users were responsible for around £1.3 billion of property crimes.

As heroin has become more easily available, so prices have fallen. By 1993 heroin was selling in London at around £80 per gramme. On the other hand, the purity and potency of both heroin and cocaine have increased. Heroin in the early 1990s was often 'cut' (contaminated) with paracetamol and caffeine. According to a study in one area of Britain, between 1982 and 1985 the average potency of street cocaine increased from 28 to 74 per cent.[21]

The spread of crack cocaine has been noted in earlier chapters, and it is important here to emphasise the social significance of this spread. As with heroin, the traffic in crack cocaine is big business, though its spread in Britain has been uneven. On 20 April 1989, Robert Stutman, senior agent of the New York Division of the Drug Enforcement Administration, addressed the Association of Chief Police Officers in Britain and predicted a crack epidemic. Within a short time, his dramatic language had been picked up by British politicians. Douglas Hurd, the then Home Secretary, called crack 'the spectre I see hanging over Europe' while Tim Eggar, then a junior minister at the Foreign Office, called it 'by far the single greatest threat that faces the UK'. In fact crack had already hit Liverpool in 1987, and it was particularly acute there in 1988.

During the following years the price of a 'rock' fell from £35 to £20. Most of the dealers were users, using mobile phones, a pattern that remains.

While cocaine use cuts across class and social divisions – the existence of cocaine groups among the aristocracy and City financiers has long been noted – the spread of crack cocaine has been most marked among poor people. Terry Williams, who has documented crack cocaine use in the USA, has stressed that it is simplistic to see this spread purely in terms of personal irresponsibility or pathology.

> Addiction did not take over people's lives because they were irresponsible or have some inherent flaw. Instead the crack users' behaviour reflected class, race and economic factors. Those who can command resources, who have the power to effect change in their lives, are very hard to find in an American Crackhouse.[22]

His comments are broadly applicable to Britain. In addition, as noted above, data from various places show that crack users as a group are often most out of touch with drugs agencies, and they are often at high risk of HIV infection.[23]

Fifthly, there is the spread of drug use into rural communities. There was a time when drug use, other than alcohol, was a mainly urban phenomenon. This has not been the case for some time. Seizures and arrests increased during 1994 in Northamptonshire, Gloucestershire and Wiltshire. North-east Scotland has the worst problem of any rural area of Britain. The fishing villages of the north-east coast of Scotland now contain more drug users per head of the population than Strathclyde, while reports of young people injecting vodka and whisky have come recently from a village in rural Yorkshire. Parts of Somerset, Devon and Cornwall have been centres of drug abuse for years. Yet sadly it would seem that many pastors and caring persons continue to regard drug problems as peculiar to the urban cores.

The sixth change is the declining role of London and the south-east and the growth of serious drug problems in the northern regions of Britain. A number of studies have suggested that the largest number of problematic drug users are now in the north and north-west of the country, and that heroin is the main drug used. Between 1981 and 1991 the number of known heroin addicts in Greater Manchester grew from 21 to 3660. A study in 1996 in the north-west of England reported that 63 per cent of users used heroin, and that 84 per cent of them were unemployed.[24] The most recent edition of the *British Crime Survey*, published on 19 September 1997, suggested that drug use was declining in London and the south but was increasing in the north and the Midlands. A study in one Glasgow school in 1995 reported that 50 per cent of pupils in one class had used heroin by the time they left.

> The drug problem now attracts far less attention from newspapers and the media in general. While this may hopefully mark the beginning of a more rational public response, it would be most dangerous to assume that the problem has been adequately dealt with.
>
> (Standing Conference on Drug Abuse, 1975)[25]
>
> Serious discussion has been allowed on most social and political issues of today – gay rights, censorship, abortion, racial discrimination and the position of women in society. But the drugs issue remains at the level of base propaganda. Any attempt at raising the level of debate is swamped by allegations of being 'soft on drugs' or condoning their use. The press retains an invidious grip on providing drug 'information' for public consumption.
>
> (Harry Shapiro, 1988)[26]

Finally, there is the issue of the media and popular culture. This last change is in many ways the most important and the most difficult to summarise briefly. It is a fact that, if it was ever the case that they were allied with a subculture in our society, today drugs are part of the culture of the mainstream. There is no part of British culture which is untouched by them. Advertising, music, art, comedy, education – all are affected in some way by drugs, irrespective of what substances are consumed by whom. *Trainspotting* was the most discussed film of 1996. Drugs permeate the language and rhetoric of the mass media. It is arguable that it is those who claim to be unaffected by this who now form the subculture.

However, with some striking exceptions, the mainstream media tends to repeat the stereotypes of the past, and does not contribute greatly to informed and creative debate on the changing place of drugs in society. A major factor here is that the world view of young people is quite different from that of the middle-aged (including their own parents). Many adults see drugs as of central importance in young people's lives, and react with a mixture of panic, fear and desire to control. Yet surveys suggest that this is not so. Most young people see jobs, social life and friends as more important than drugs, but they accept drugs as part of the normal life of society (in contrast to the middle-aged who often see them as 'deviant' and out of the mainstream). The widely reported comment by Noel Gallagher of Oasis that for many people taking drugs was the equivalent of having a cup of tea, however shocking to some, was in fact perfectly true as a statement of fact.[27] Yet much adult rhetoric on the subject is light years away from the reality of young people's lives. It is only when this global generation gulf is recognised for what it is that real communication can begin again.

So the social structure of Britain's drug-using communities has changed, and a number of consequences flow from this. The most obvious change is statistical: there are now far more drug users per head of the population than has been the case for some time. As drug use has spread, the 'typical' drug user has become more 'ordinary', and it is increasingly misleading to try to describe drug use as a sign of personal pathology. Most drug use is well within the cultural conformities of the west. Drug users are more and more like everybody else.

6

Pastoral Care and the Role of the Christian Community

> It's a long road to Canaan
> On Bleecker Street.
>
> (Paul Simon)[1]
>
> What we call pastoral care should be reconceived as a practical theology of care, and should address not only the pastoral care of those within the church but also attempt to both criticise and fulfil the care structures of the larger society.
>
> (Don Browning, 1985)[2]
>
> Be a shepherd of a flock doomed to slaughter.
>
> (Zechariah 11:4, NRSV)

Some issues for pastoral care

It is, of course, impossible to separate the questions of pastoral care of drug users and their families from those of pastoral care as a whole, and this book cannot deal with the whole question of the changing shape of pastoral ministry in the churches. However, two recent developments seem to be of particular importance in relation to drug use. The first is the massive increase in pastoral counselling agencies and in individuals offering this kind of personal service activity, usually in exchange for payment. The second is the apparent decline in many places in street ministry and in the accessibility of priests and ministers at the level of street work. Within the churches, to some extent, this shift has gone hand in hand with the growth of lay ministry and the 'declericalising' of pastoral work, and it has also been linked with the growth of secular agencies within, for example, the youth service. To that extent it should be welcomed, but there are some serious dangers which I will refer to below. One of them can be summed up as follows: in pastoral care as a whole, and in the field of ministry to drug users, as forms of 'service provision' have increased in some areas, increasing numbers of people are now cut off from all of them.

Again, the field of drug use is one of many where a multi-disciplinary and holistic response is crucial, yet often this does not happen. Churches, organisations with a social work or health service background, youth workers, general practitioners, needle exchanges, therapeutic communities and many others often pursue their own approach as if it were the only one available. There is no evidence that the churches are more guilty of this than anyone else, and much evidence to the contrary. Indeed, church members have been active in the field for a long time even though church members as a whole remain fairly ignorant of what is going on. Nevertheless, the field of drug use calls for co-operation between disciplines, and for the transgression of conventional boundaries both of discourse and of practice.

This raises the whole question of drug users themselves, their rights, opinions, contribution, expertise and need to organise. There has been an increase in recent years in Britain in the formation of addicts' rights groups and unions, and there is a need to develop more networks in which drug users can make their voices heard on the lines of Street Voice in Baltimore, or Outside in Portland, USA, or similar groups in European cities. But it is still very common, indeed the norm, that the problems of drug takers are discussed by others in their absence: the drug user is someone who is the recipient of other people's plans and actions.

In recent years, in response to government strategy, Drug Action Teams (DATs) and Drug Reference Groups (DRGs) – the latter a more open and enlarged development from the former – have been set up in many areas. One of the intentions of these groups was that the views of users should be heard and reflected. However, both the Drug Action Teams and the Drug Reference Groups are usually dominated by local professionals, and drug users themselves are not represented.

Indeed, according to one recent study of 457 drug-service users, only 15 per cent of Drug Reference Groups had any drug users represented. A total of 88 per cent of the drug users interviewed did not know what a Drug Reference Group was, and of those who claimed to know, most were wrong, believing it to be a referral agency![3] In some areas, members of the DRG have complained that they know nothing about the members of the DAT, and that the DAT seems cut off from much local work in the field.

It is against this somewhat frustrating background, within which nonetheless much has been achieved, that we need to consider the role of churches. It is obvious that churches need to function within the specific context in which they are set, and they can only effectively do so if they are aware of what is happening. Yet it is by no means clear that this is so. A recent study of the role of faith communities in Croydon commented on the local religious leaders:

> The leaders of all the religious communities were aware that drug abuse existed in Croydon although none of them had any personal experience or knew of anyone who was affected . . . None of the leaders had any real knowledge.[4]

It is of vital importance, if churches are to become more involved in pastoral care of drug users, that they are well-informed and aware of what is going on. The task of adequate education for church leaders at every level is fundamental. This includes education about drug use among church members. A study of 7666 young people by the Evangelical Coalition on Drugs at the Spring Harvest festival in 1995 suggested that there was almost as much drug use among young people within churches as among the unchurched.

Drug prevention and education can take place only if there is close contact with people at risk, and if there is a real understanding of the situation, and this involves enlisting the help of informed young people within all decision-making processes and planning of strategies. Local churches are in a potentially strong position to take part in such work, and no doubt many of them are already involved.

Assuming that there is such awareness, how are local churches likely to be involved? There are three main areas which are important, and have been for many years: educational and preventive work; social support, including outreach and crisis ministries; and after-care.[5]

Educational and preventive work

> Children may be ignorant but they are not stupid. When the evidence of their own experience contradicts adult propaganda, they (like sensible adults) rely on their own experience – and tend in the future to distrust a source of information which they had found unreliable in the past.
>
> (E Brecher, 1990)[6]

The issues of drug prevention and education have been matters of concern since the mid-1960s, but it is only recently that governments have begun to take them seriously, though, many would say, in a half-hearted way. The former Prime Minister, John Major, spoke in 1992 of the need for 'ever-improving prevention'. So, after years of stressing that 'prevention is better than cure', many drugs workers feel that there now seems a possibility that the message is getting through, although far more is still spent on enforcement and control than on prevention and education. (In 1993–4, for example, £209 million was spent on the former compared with £104 million on the latter.) Yet the government has, it seems, come round to a recognition of the importance of preventive work. However, it is not at all clear that the meaning of prevention is understood, and the word is used very loosely and vaguely. The Treaty of European Union, for example, contains no definition of prevention in spite of its insistence (in Article 129) that the fight against drugs is important.

So what is preventive work? And does it prevent? The idea still persists in many quarters that the dissemination of accurate information is all that is required. The research on drug education has not been able to show the extent to which such efforts have significant effects on future drug use, but it is certainly clear that simply communicating 'facts' alone is unhelpful. A report in 1972 stressed that drug information had become big business in the USA and had produced thousands of drug 'experts', but that it hadn't worked, and might have made things worse.[7] It is necessary to focus on such areas as behaviour change, the acquiring of life skills and not simply cerebral knowledge. Again, this is an area where the church could play a major role, and it has implications which go way beyond the field of drug education. The church is one of the main bodies in British society which takes adult education seriously, and this expertise needs to be mobilised in relation to drugs. There are fundamental issues here about the nature of education, the nature of the human person, and the character of a truthful and truth-seeking community. The work of drug prevention is more about creating a caring and truthful environment than it is about putting obstacles in the way of drug use.

Since the 1960s there have been many examples of groups who have approached drug problems from the perspective of prevention. The Maze Project, based in Bethnal Green, works on drug prevention and education in the East End of London. It grew out of work done over many years by detached youth workers, particularly at Avenues Unlimited. Like Avenues, it is under the general auspices of the Young Women's Christian Association (YWCA) but has a high degree of autonomy, its own management committee, and so on. Over the last eight or so years the project has developed work in primary and secondary schools, with families, youth workers and tenants' groups, with peer education, and more recently with the growing numbers of young prostitutes in the Whitechapel area. (The work of the Marigold Project, referred to in the previous chapter, grew out of the Maze's work.) The Maze Project is the only group in the area working almost entirely in the field of education and prevention, though many agencies and groups are involved at the level of treatment, support and help for established addicts. The Maze Project is primarily concerned with helping young people not to get to that stage, with prevention rather than 'cure', with education and help at an early stage.

The Maze Project has never believed in scare tactics and is careful to avoid exaggeration which can lead to a deep mistrust in all drug information emanating from adult sources. It recognises that there is already drug 'information' among children as young as six or seven. While care is needed to avoid giving children information which they cannot handle, or in putting material into their minds at too early a stage, it is equally important to be aware and responsive when children have already acquired ideas, often incorrect and misleading ideas, from other sources.

The Maze workers do not treat drug education in isolation from education for life within society. They see 'prevention' in the old-English sense of 'going before', preparing the ground on which mature, informed and healthy options may be chosen. With two full-time workers and a fairly small budget, the Maze Project offers a model which could be developed in many other areas, and in which local churches could play an important role.

Social support, outreach and crisis ministry

> The only people I found who were willing to go into these places that were dangerous and dirty and detracting, and work with these kids in one-to-one outreach ministries, were people of faith.
>
> (John Dilulio, 1997)[8]
>
> You need to have a certain type of personality. You need to know the streets and to understand the culture before you can establish any trust. So far there is little evidence that drug services will employ staff who are able to do that.
>
> (Lyn Matthews, 1992)[9]

A second area is what I term social support, outreach and crisis ministry. This begins by a recognition that many people have, by the time we contact them, already passed certain stages of danger, and that to speak purely in terms of 'prevention' is naive and unrealistic. It is clear that there is a massive problem in Britain and elsewhere of marginalisation, of people and communities who are pushed to the edge of society, and a corresponding problem of how pastoral ministry in this context is to be defended and extended. The current government uses the term 'social exclusion' and has set up a unit to respond to it. Others use the language of 'underclass'. Many of these terms are problematic, but what is important is to recognise and try to respond to the existence of major fissures and areas of social fragmentation within our society. At a pastoral level, it means that churches and caring agencies are at this point cut off from many groups and individuals, often including those who use illicit drugs.

However, it seems to be the case that in many areas the close links at street level which detached youth workers, sometimes associated with local churches or Christian organisations, and some priests and ministers once had, are no longer so evident, and many drug users are slipping through all the pastoral support systems. There is considerable evidence that thousands of drug users are not known to established agencies. In one part of South London, for example, while £4 million had been spent in each year on drug services, only one-third of cocaine users had any contact with services, while other research suggests that most methadone programmes only reach about 20 per cent of the addict population in most countries.[10]

Counselling, however, usually depends for its effectiveness on adequate networks of contact and referral, and the data do seem to suggest that there is often a breakdown at the level of primary contact. All the counselling, referrals, detoxification programmes, and so on will not avail if the initial contact has not been made. Hence the importance of what is called 'outreach'.

The notion of 'outreach' goes back to the 1860s, and has been recently revived, particularly in connection with HIV and AIDS work. The term is used equally, though with different connotations, by evangelical Christians and by secular professionals in the drugs field. In relation to drugs work, it has been defined as 'any community-orientated activity aiming to contact individuals and groups not regularly in contact with existing services'.[11] However, much of what is termed 'outreach' does not in fact reach those who are completely alienated and disconnected from service provision or from established agencies and institutions. The local church does need to get back to the streets, to the districts of infection and the sites of crisis, and to be present where the pain is. More will be said about this, but it needs to be emphasised at this point that if the local church, clergy and laity, has no points of contact with the street drug taker, the ability to be of use will be limited to a few areas and to those points where the drug user moves towards them. These can be important, but the primary point of entry at street level has been lost in many places.

In recent work with drug users, one of the most frequently used terms is 'harm reduction'. The idea of harm reduction has been a central one in drug work since the 1960s, but its recent popularising has been related to the spread of HIV and AIDS. However, while there is considerable evidence that these efforts have led to 'safer sex' among gay men, it is not so clear that this is the case among intravenous drug users. Certainly harm-reduction strategies have led to safer injecting, but sexual behaviour has changed less among addicts. Contrary to some myths, most drug users are sexually active, many change partners frequently, and there is considerable contact between users and non-users. There is still much work to be done in this area.[12]

The growth of harm-reduction strategies is international, and is based on the principle that, while abstinence and 'a completely new way of life' may be desirable, they are not possible for large numbers of people at this point in time. Should they be abandoned? Those committed to a philosophy of harm reduction begin with the practical recognition that we cannot simply wait until people are where we want them to be. We must begin where people actually are. This means taking risks, accepting that perfection may not be an immediate goal, accepting too that we may have to use unusual methods and be ready for innovative strategies. Thus in Berlin, Utrecht and other cities, there are cafés for drug-dependent prostitutes which provide legal, medical and social help. In Oslo, two prostitutes have been employed by the Directorate of Health to do outreach work. From a Christian theological perspective, the fundamental principle here is one of incarnational presence, a presence which is humble and willing to live with imperfection, limitation and untidiness.[13]

It is important to say something here about what is called detached youth work and its relevance to Christian ministry. Beginning in the 1950s, the Teddy Boy era, with work such as that of the Teen Canteen in the Elephant and Castle district of South London, detached youth work developed particularly in Inner London in the 1960s with projects such as the Hoxton Café Project, the Portobello Project, the Soho Project, and Avenues Unlimited. The main characteristic of detached work was the practice of youth work without premises, although usually an office was a feature of the youth worker's structure. Much of the youth worker's time was spent in bars, amusement arcades, clubs and in the streets, making contacts with young people who were 'unattached'. The earlier term 'unclubbables' was based on the spurious notion that most young people went to clubs, whereas in fact the unattached were, and are, the majority!

One of the earliest detached youth workers, Barbara Ward, said in 1969:

> At some point, when the young person is sufficiently diseased, pitifully broken down, we all rally, and enormous resources are put at his feet. If he gets close to the point of self-destruction, or suicide, or turns his back on society, we will help. But if he is just slightly feckless, lazy, using a few drugs, we are not interested.[14]

Youth workers are invariably the people most directly in touch with young people at risk. They are trained and experienced in street work, and adapt quickly to new situations. They are often local people themselves. Their length of stay in an area is quite dramatically greater than that of some other professionals who come and go at great speed. They are less bogged down with excessive paper, jargon, and the paraphernalia of the bureaucratic state machine. They can operate in unconventional ways. Through their ability to be flexible, to work unsocial hours, and to remain in post for a long time, detached youth workers have often been the first and main point of contact for the street drug user. Christian groups, such as the YWCA, which set up Avenues Unlimited in East London and the Manningham Project in Bradford, or local churches, such as those which set up the Leeds City Centre Detached Youth Work Project, or David Randall's work at St Botolph's, Aldgate, have been in the forefront of detached youth work for many years. Today, as whole areas of youth culture and alienation have undergone massive shifts, the whole concept and approach of detached work must be rethought. But in its essential features it remains of absolutely critical importance.[15]

Today we are in a situation of immense social chaos in which the skills of the detached youth work tradition are needed more than ever. One well-informed observer has recently claimed that 'detached work may have to become the norm rather than the exception for any agency purporting to offer a service to crack users'.[16] Again, the shift to dance drugs has had important effects on the character and style of drug-related counselling and has made it more important for workers to be able to operate at a level which is more chaotic and less structured.

One of the main emphases in youth work has been on 'informal education'. If the primary foundation of informal education in the drugs field is missing at the local level, then later attempts at containment or cure can be very expensive and achieve little. If this work does not occur, we will be spending billions on treatment and much of it will be wasted. Yet today detached work, like the youth service as a whole, is in acute crisis. Five years ago one national newspaper claimed that 'the country's entire youth service is facing dissolution', and quoted the General Secretary of the Youth and Community Workers' Union, 'We expect the demise of the youth service by next year'.[17] This has not occurred, but the position is very serious, and must be of urgent concern to all churches.

As an example of Christian ministry among drug users which combined detached work, education and other forms of crisis ministry within an area of high infection, it is worth considering the work of St Anne's House, Soho, in the late 1960s and early 1970s. Soho, the district of London's West End, south of Oxford Street, north-east of Piccadilly, north of Leicester Square, and west of Charing Cross Road, has long been a mecca for minority groups. At the end of the seventeenth century the parish was 45 per cent French. In 1953 the first espresso coffee machine in England was set up in Soho, while 1957 saw the beginning of the Carnaby Street culture with the opening of John Stephens' shop.

Soho in 1967 was at the heart of the drug culture not only of London but of Britain. The Haymarket exit of Piccadilly Circus Underground Station, adjacent to the all-night Boots chemist, was known as 'junkies' corner', and the term 'Piccadilly junkie' was coming into use.[18] Nearby was Playland, an amusement arcade, which was notorious both for drug dealing and for male prostitution, and figured in the television documentary 'Johnny Go Home'. It was here in 1963 that the 'pep pill' crisis was recognised by the media. The coffee clubs and bars off Wardour Street were well-known centres of amphetamine traffic. The two main pubs used by heroin addicts were just north of Soho in the Goodge Street area.

A group of us set up the Soho Drugs Group in 1967. At first it was based in an all-night coffee club within the main area of amphetamine dealing. The club had a welfare committee including a priest (myself), a lawyer, a probation officer, and a nurse from the local VD clinic. We felt strongly that since most young drug takers used the clubs, it was important to base such work within the club culture itself. Later, when the group was established, we moved its base to St Anne's House, the centre of the local parish.

Our work at St Anne's included formal and informal education, pastoral work in the clubs, bars and amusement arcades, the creation of a spiritual centre, a training base, a place of prayer and spiritual guidance, and providing a link between the street addict and resources of help elsewhere. Piccadilly, described by one journalist in 1969 as 'full of loneliness', was at the centre of our detached work, and it was here that the term 'detached priest' was first used in the same period.[19]

At almost the same time as the work at St Anne's got under way, Kaleidoscope began in 1968 at John Bunyan Baptist Church in Kingston-on-Thames. Its original base was an all-night Friday club with music and food. Like St Anne's, one of its central concerns has been with harm minimisation. It provides a drop-in clinic run by a consultant psychiatrist, doctors and nurses, a methadone scheme with a computerised dispensing programme, a needle exchange used by 300 addicts, free condoms, a 24-hour drugs helpline, a hostel and a small detoxification unit. Not all the workers are Christians, though the basis of the project is very clearly so. Today Kaleidoscope is still primarily a club with a clinic inside it. It is an excellent example of a local church responding to the needs of the community. The founder, Eric Blakebrough, speaks of 'rehabilitation before detoxification', recognising that pastoral care, including 'after-care', may start at many points.[20] Today many Christian and other groups draw on the experience and expertise of Kaleidoscope as a foundation for their own response to local needs.

As a third example of crisis ministry we may consider Mission on the Margins. Now a national network, this movement grew from the work of a remarkable woman, Mary Beasley, in Birmingham. Mary, a disabled woman and former social worker, had been working with homeless and alcoholic people, as well as with other marginal groups, for some years. Through writing a university thesis on her work, she came into contact with a wide range of people doing similar work in other towns and cities. Out of this grew a national network, which brought together a diverse group of people from all the churches, including many who themselves are marginal to the institution, and who share a common commitment to service and to advocacy on behalf of those who have been cast off or rejected by the system.

Mission on the Margins combines individual and community-based work with marginal groups and in marginal forms of ministry with a network of support, reflection and mutual strengthening. At a time when more people are being pushed to the edges of society, and when many carers are under extreme physical, psychological and spiritual pressure, the work of this kind of network is vital.[21]

After-care

The earliest after-care centre for drug addicts in Britain was established by the Community of St Mary the Virgin at Spelthorne St Mary in the nineteenth century. During the 1960s many of the centres were run by evangelical Christian groups, such as the New Life Centre in Bromley, Life for the World in Blockley, Moreton-in-Marsh, and the Coke Hole Trust, based in the Andover area. The Coke Hole Trust grew out of the Billy Graham Crusade of the 1960s when Doug and Barbara Henry met their first heroin addicts in Soho, and brought one of them to share their home life in a Hampshire village. From this small beginning developed the major after-care facility which is the Coke Hole today. Some of the others have collapsed through lack of funding, though newer ones, such as Yeldall Manor in Berkshire, have developed.

One of the areas of disagreement among Christian after-care groups is around the external paraphernalia associated with drug use. One of the early pentecostal organisations working with drug users, the Full Gospel Business Men's Voice, once produced a 'before and after' poster. In the first picture was a 'beatnik' with long hair, beads, colourful jacket and psychedelic shirt. Next to it was a picture of the same man after conversion.

He was wearing a sports jacket and tie, and had short hair and 'Palmolive' complexion, the epitome of middle-class suburban Christianity. Not all of the evangelical groups agreed with the philosophy underlying this poster which clearly associated Christianity with a particular cultural style. However, some groups take the view that, for recovery to occur, there needs to be a clean break not only with drugs but also with all the cultural accompaniments of drug use. So at Yeldall Manor, and at the associated Yeldall Christian Centres, leather jackets and certain kinds of jewellery, T-shirts, hairstyles and records are banned. The theory behind this is that drug use will not come to an end through determination or willpower but only through the creation of a new lifestyle, new friends and a new support structure.

The role of evangelical Christian groups in after-care is only one facet of evangelical work in this field which has been evident since the early 1960s. Most of the British evangelical groups were initially inspired by David Wilkerson's book *The Cross and the Switchblade* and its account of the work of Teen Challenge in the USA. Much of the literature associated with these groups is extremely anecdotal and often inaccurate. As with many other groups, some of the evangelicals make exaggerated claims and are weak on factual accuracy. Some groups demand such high motivation at the point of entry to their programme that they exclude most drug users from the outset, and they can be highly intolerant of others, including other Christians, who have different approaches. However, there is no doubt that much of the work done by these groups is very dedicated, deeply rooted, and has an abiding and rock-like character.[22] In recent years some new evangelical groups have emerged, and, in an attempt to provide some co-ordination for these groups, the Evangelical Coalition on Drugs was set up in 1989.

Of course, many after-care groups are not Christian though some of them have a quasi-monastic character with a clear ideology, corporate discipline and rules of behaviour. Synanon, the pioneer of therapeutic communities in the field of drugs other than alcohol, was founded in 1958. In the 1980s a series of claims about sexual harassment, violence and the authoritarian style of the leadership signalled the beginning of the end of the movement. (These are recurring problems in the field, and are worthy of further study.) But out of Synanon grew the Phoenix Houses and other similar communities.

The model for many after-care groups is Alcoholics Anonymous (AA), founded in Akron, Ohio in 1935, and heavily influenced by the Oxford Group which became Moral Rearmament. There is no doubt that AA works for many, but it should not be viewed as an adequate model for all people or for all time, or as the only way of salvation from addiction. Much of the language of AA is open to question and scrutiny. Of the Twelve Steps, ten are based on the Oxford Group. The influence of AA has been enormous, particularly in the USA, where it is often seen as the uniquely American contribution to spirituality, and the language of the 'Twelve Steps' has entered into the vocabulary of care and counselling. Many people now use terms like control, recovery and denial, though some see the danger of a new kind of 'recovery fundamentalism'.[23]

The whole field of after-care is a difficult one, not least from the perspective of funding (see Chapter Eight). There are questions too about power, freedom and maturity. There is no doubt that a rigid, authoritarian regime works for many people, though there is debate about whether this in itself perpetuates immaturity and unhealthy dependence. However, it is equally clear that such programmes simply do not help many individuals, and that after-care – as indeed does pastoral work as a whole – needs to be immensely diverse in its approaches and methods.[24]

The Christian ministry in the field of drug use and addiction raises many of the key theological ideas about sin, grace, human will, the world, and the Kingdom of God, which divide Christians, and it also offers a possible creative site for working through them ecumenically in co-operative action and praxis-based reflection. There is not space here to engage in a detailed theological examination of all these themes, but several of them are worth noting.

First, there is the concept of addiction and its relationship with humanity and human sin. Although addiction is conventionally seen in terms of sickness, there has been a trend recently in some circles to see addiction as a form or manifestation of original sin. 'Everyone is an addict of something' has become a fashionable concept, not only among Christians. The words 'addiction' and 'addictive' have become clichés and thought-substitutes in much writing. The context in which addiction arises is often ignored, so that the focus comes to be exclusively on personal sin, and on the addict as one trapped within the addictive prison. There is a tendency to equate victim and perpetrator. But, leaving aside whether sin and addiction can be equated, sin cannot be reduced to a single cause. There is a need to distinguish sin from victimisation. There is a self-surrender which is due to coercion or convention, as well as self-surrender willingly to a drug, or, under different circumstances, to the will of God. Here the Catholic stress on context, on the process of sanctification, and on detail and particularity can help us to avoid harmful generalities.

Secondly, what kind of God do we believe in? The view of God which is found in some religious groups working with addiction issues is often that of a dictator and controller. God can easily be portrayed as an alternative, albeit better, form of addiction.[25] Christians need to be careful that we do not offer a diminished and trivialised understanding of God as a response to drugs. When Marx called religion an opiate, he was making an important observation – and a warning.

Thirdly, it is important to stress that there is no specific 'ministry to drug users'. The use of drugs raises specific questions and problems, but Christian ministry is to all people. The modern habit of labelling people (client, addict, alcoholic, and so on) does not fit well with the Christian view of what it is to be human or with the doctrine of the Body of Christ in which all are equal. Nevertheless, the field of drugs can help to illuminate neglected areas of ministry and help us towards a clearer understanding.

Finally, there is a central place for silence, darkness and the way of 'unknowing'. Pastoral ministry in the drug field calls for a profound spiritual rootedness in God, and for those essentially priestly tasks of eucharistic sacrifice and adoration, intercession, and solidarity in Christ through the sharing of silence and darkness. I emphatically do not mean that these are tasks only for ordained priests, but rather that it is here that the priestly character of the whole Church, in which, of course, ordained priests and ministers have an important role, is most clearly revealed. This largely hidden dimension of the Body of Christ is of particularly central significance in a field such as drug addiction where it is not possible, much of the time, to see the prospect of immediate change, and it is important to stay with the pain, the wounds, the brokenness, the repeated crises and the darkness, in faith and trust.

Sacramental ministry, including the ministry of anointing and deliverance, is important in this area, and both laying on of hands and anointing should be exercised, with due care and preparation, but frequently and repeatedly. Often sacramental ministry, which relies on symbolic objectivity rather than on personal feeling or intellectual argument will be of greater value than anything else.

The experience of work in the field of drug use can help to illuminate the nature of priesthood and of sacrifice. It can help to bring out more deeply the inner reality of life in Christ. For the roots of priesthood, of the sacrificial ministry of the Church, lie in the redemptive work of Christ. In his book *A Theology of Auschwitz*, Ulrich Simon defines priesthood as 'the office which ritually, inwardly and ascetically shares the dying and rising of Christ'. In the context of the concentration camp, when the priest is without status and function, without bread and wine, the sacrificial heart of priesthood is laid bare, its essential character exposed.

> The priestly ideal uses and converts the nothingness which the world of Auschwitz offers. Here the priest's sacerdotal dedication encounters the vacuum with self-sacrifice . . . The priest at the camp counts because he has no desires of self-importance and gives life because he stands already beyond extermination. He is the exact opposite of the king rat. The hour of darkness cannot take him by surprise since he has practised silence in darkness.[26]

His reflection has profound significance in relation to work with drug users. Much ministry in the drug scene is marked by darkness, silence and uncertainty. It calls us to an apophatic style of pastoral care in which clarity and method give way to waiting and 'unknowing'.[27] It calls us to recover some very traditional themes – the spirit of sacrifice, the theme of priesthood as an interior life not simply a job, the emphasis on ascetical discipline and on the practice of the Christian life. The priestly ministry is concerned with the work of intercession, of healing, of reconciliation, and this calls for a profound inner *ascesis*, a dark night of the soul, a sharing in Christ's dying and rising. In a world where many die alone and abandoned, the central task of the Church is to share that darkness and be a powerful witness to life beyond the tombs.

The experience of pastoral care in the drug scene is one which illuminates and reinforces the importance of stability and persistence through times which seem hopeless and bleak. It is not an experience of quick fixes or of band-aid ministry though it certainly includes this as an important element in the total picture. But it is an experience of sharing in the revolutionary patience of the God who transcends time, and who will heal and transform in strange and unexpected ways. Our task is to be faithful and attentive.

7

The Drug Culture and Spirituality

The spiritual significance of drug use

> To many Christians the idea that the drug scene might have 'religious' or 'spiritual' significance will be quite monstrous.
>
> (Kenneth Leech, 1972)[1]
>
> . . . the alienated young are giving shape to something that looks like the saving vision our endangered civilisation requires.
>
> (Theodore Roszak, 1970)[2]

'To many Christians the idea that the drug scene might have "religious" or "spiritual" significance will be quite monstrous.' I wrote those words twenty-five years ago, and they are still broadly true. The idea of an association between drugs and spirituality still seems almost indecent to many people, yet the evidence, both historical and pastoral, that it is so is overwhelming. Many Christians still see drug-using communities as wholly decadent and find the notion that there is any kind of 'spirituality' there abhorrent and offensive and incomprehensible. Many church groups assume that drug users are peculiarly and uniquely sinful, and mobilise their resources accordingly. Here there is no idea that drug cultures might have spiritual aspects. So in 1969 one Christian group offered material which, it said, was 'relevant to teenagers drifting into a sin-stained psychedelic world of drugs and drink'.[3] This kind of language is still common, but it is as pastorally and factually indefensible as is the view that all drug users are engaged in a conscious spiritual quest.

I want to argue that much drug use, and much of the motivation for drug use, is connected with the search for meaning, for identity, for the 'beyond within', and for what has come to be known as 'spirituality'. As such it should neither be despised nor sentimentalised. Here there is space only to identify some of the main issues which need to be recognised if churches, and their priests and pastors, are to play a role other than that of social service provider.

The first is the fact that, in one sense, the use of drugs to attain 'spiritual' experiences or to find meaning in life is simply an extension of the conventional western idea of 'better living through chemistry'. For many years western people, particularly in the USA, have assumed that there is a chemical solution to every human problem, while minorities, rejecting this dominant view, have adopted a strongly anti-physical approach to health and sickness. An area in which this conflict has come to the fore dramatically is in the debates over schizophrenia and conditions such as depression or anxiety. Research has been taking place for many years into a possible chemical basis for psychosis, and recent years have seen major advances in the treatment of depression and anxiety through the use of chemicals affecting the central nervous system. There are 'fundamentalists' on both sides, those who have an uncritical faith in chemical means, and those who reject all chemical-based approaches in favour of therapeutic work or other means of a drug-free kind. It is a logical step to extend this conflict to the area of spiritual experience, to believe that spiritual truths and remedies can also be found through use of the appropriate pill, or, conversely, to repudiate all such approaches.

In fact, drugs have been used for religious purposes for thousands of years, from the inhaling of vapours in ancient Delphi onwards. (There is a vague reference in Proverbs 27:9 to the inhaling of perfumes.) In recent western history, earlier twentieth-century movements had used drugs for religious purposes. There were clear religious ideas in the beats of the Kerouac generation who combined cannabis use and a fascination with Zen. 'The beat seeks the salvation of his soul', wrote one anarchist commentator in 1962[4]. Cannabis also figured in groups involved with the occult such as Aleister Crowley (1875–1947) who claimed that it showed 'that there exists another world attainable – somehow'.[5]

Secondly, while there had been an interest in the area for some time, the mass interest in opening up new levels of consciousness through psychoactive drugs was a product of the growth of the counter-culture of the late 1960s. The counter-culture opened up the whole field of approaches to consciousness, and initiated a new epoch of thought and feeling in the west. Drugs were an important element in this process. These were also the years when R. D. Laing was pointing out that many people were seeking what he called 'meta-egoic' experiences, experiences of transcendence of ordinary waking consciousness, and were prepared to go to great lengths to achieve such experiences. Laing believed that people engaging in such a journey needed maps of the meta-egoic world, and they went to texts such as *The Tibetan Book of the Dead*, the *I Ching*, and *The Secret of the Golden Flower*.[6] On the whole, they bypassed the Christian tradition, assuming that it had nothing to say to them.

The counter-culture of the 1960s had major effects on the approach to spirituality.[7] Many hippies saw the churches as very unspiritual indeed and unaware of the spiritual currents of the time. Caroline Coon saw the hippie as protesting against 'a society whose moral spirit is lower and more disillusioned than it has been for a long time'.[8] While the original hippie movement faded within a few years, the view that those years have left no abiding legacy is very unimaginative and lacking in perception.

Thirdly, it seems clear that mainstream churches are not meeting the widespread need for ecstasy, for transcendence and for mystery. The name 'ecstasy', given to a range of drugs used at raves, is not accidental, for it indicates a quest for moments of ecstasy, moments when the individual is taken outside of the conventional waking self, and merges with the crowd in some kind of corporate consciousness. It was this kind of experience which religious gatherings once provided, and in some communities still do. It was the sense of the need for some kind of religious expression of, and within, the rave culture which led to the Nine O'clock Service in Sheffield. It would be appalling if the serious issues of the abuse of power and sexual harassment which arose there obscured the ongoing need for reflection on the religious issues involved.[9]

Fourthly, we need to recognise that many young people have, after taking psychedelic drugs, moved beyond reliance on the drug-induced experience. The term 'meta-hippies' seems to have been coined by Allan Y. Cohen many years ago as a way of describing those who had moved beyond the use of psychedelic drugs. They have made what Cohen termed the 'journey beyond trips'.[10] This quest has been going on now for over thirty years. It is evident in many of the 'new spiritual movements'.

The journey eastwards and the quest for a global community

> The people of the east are our friends. We are much more like them than we are like the average westerner, and, because they are much closer to the truth, they can be turned on much easier, and also there is so much we can learn from them. We, who are out there, should communicate with all people, good and bad, and so strengthen the bond between us and the east.
>
> (Jim Griffin, 1968)[11]

Part of the counter-culture interest in spiritual issues was the fascination with the religions of the east. At the end of the 1960s Roszak had noted 'the strong influence on the young of Eastern religions'.[12] Linked with this has been the sense of entering a new age of consciousness, a new age of the spirit. Many of the post-1960s spiritual seekers speak of the 'Age of Aquarius' or the 'Aquarian frontier', a world in which ecology, the psychic, 'wild science', and 'free-wheeling religiosity' flourish. 'This is the dawning of the Age of Aquarius', announced the 1960s musical *Hair.* Some say that we entered it in 1904, while others look to the year 3000. Some speak of two phases – 1846–1918 and 1918–90, with a complete transformation by 2062. For many February 1962 is an important date when Jupiter came into alignment with Mars, Mercury, Venus, Saturn, and the sun and moon.

Since then we have had New Age movements in which there is a mingling of eastern mysticism, new physics and transpersonal psychology.[13] The origins of the present fascination with the theme of a 'New Age' lie in the counter-cultural movements of the 1960s, though its antecedents lie in earlier mystical and visionary trends. For the most part, these movements have little interest in drugs of a synthetic kind, but their rejection of dominant western technocracy (of which drug consumption is a major element) is more fundamental. While one wing of New Age has rejected the drug route altogether, there are many for whom use of mind-changing substances is part of a quest for personal and social transformation and for a more holistic and global consciousness.

Psychedelic drugs and mystical experience

> A psychedelic experience is a journey to new realms of consciousness . . . Such experiences of enlarged consciousness can occur in a variety of ways: sensory deprivation, yoga exercises, disciplined meditation, religious or aesthetic ecstasies, or spontaneously. Most recently they have become available to anyone through the ingestion of psychedelic drugs such as LSD, psilocybin, mescaline, DMT, etc.
>
> (Timothy Leary *et al*, 1965)[14]
>
> Do you really think that the 'gates of perception' open cold to a nit like you as a consequence of sucking a Tate and Lyle cube impregnated with a Swiss chemical?
>
> (Colin MacInnes, 1967)[15]

A central issue in the spread of LSD has been the claim that psychedelic chemicals can help to produce experiences which are identical, or closely comparable, to those described in the mystical texts. What does this claim mean?

In the accounts of experiences of transcendence within the classical mystical tradition, there are a number of consistent features: a sense of oneness with God and/or the universe; a transcendence of time and space; an insight into the meaning of reality; a sense of awe and mystery, and ineffability; an experience of joy and peace; and lasting effects on ongoing life.

The claim that such an experience can be induced by drugs has been expressed by a number of western thinkers since the beginning of the twentieth century. William James in 1902, who experimented with nitrous oxide, claimed that he had received an insight which had metaphysical significance, especially in relation to the reconciliation of opposites and contradictions. All the issues raised by LSD were detailed in a pamphlet cited by James in 1902, Benjamin Paul Blood's *The Anaesthetic Revelation and the Gist of Philosophy* (1874). The idea is that there are screens and filters which prevent access to deeper realms or levels of consciousness and that these are temporarily lifted by the use of drugs.

Later Aldous Huxley made similar claims for the use of mescalin to which he had been introduced by Humphry Osmond. This substance, he claimed, could cleanse 'the doors of perception'. When Huxley first took mescalin in 1953, he claimed to have seen what Adam saw on the first day of creation. Believing that human beings would always need 'artificial paradises', he referred to the 'chemical conditions of transcendental experience'. Huxley became a key figure in the modern history of the use of drugs for spiritual or quasi-spiritual reasons. The rock group The Doors named themselves after his book *The Doors of Perception,* while The Beatles put his portrait on the cover of their *Sergeant Pepper* album.[16]

One of the most important and influential writers in this area was the late Alan Watts, an ex-Anglican priest turned drug–Zen teacher. According to Watts, LSD helps people to discover the central human experience, known in Zen as *satori* and in Hinduism as *moksha,* an experience which changes all others, and brings about a cosmic consciousness. There is, he argues, no essential difference between the experiences with or without the aid of chemicals, and he even suggests that LSD should be taken in a retreat house under the guidance of a spiritual director.[17]

Some recent Christian thinkers, such as Walter Pahnke, who conducted an experiment with theological students on LSD on Good Friday, have claimed that some LSD experiences do contain all the features of the classical religious experiences. Pahnke's work was carried out at Harvard University where, in the early 1960s a good deal of experimentation had been taking place involving psilocybin and LSD. People had reported mystical experiences of transcendence of time sense, experience of several levels of being, and so on. Pahnke sought to test these within the context of a faith community.[18]

Another figure who needs to be considered in relation to the link between psychedelic drugs and spiritual experience is the evangelical psychiatrist Frank Lake, founder of the school of Clinical Theology. Lake used LSD in therapy, and described how, when using the drug himself, he was plunged into a 'glorious liberating experience' of monistic identification with the life of the womb. He felt that he had experienced God as the ground of his being, and used terms such as sheer bliss, and life without ego boundaries.[19] Lake was for a time extremely influential in Christian circles in Britain, and his work, while eccentric and at times lacking in sophistication, is of central importance in studying the frontiers of pharmacology, mental illness and spirituality. His commitment to LSD was, in my view, central, rather than peripheral, to his life and thought, and he was something of a fundamentalist in his approach to it.

It has been suggested, and the statistical evidence seems to support the view, that the LSD-induced mystical experience leans towards some form of pantheism unless there are religious images already established. Many LSD users have moved in the direction of Hinduism, sometimes combining their religious position with continued use of the drug, sometimes abandoning drug use altogether. A number of the early members of the Krishna Consciousness movement in London were former LSD users, and that movement took a sympathetic approach to former drug users, combined with an essentially hostile attitude to the continued use of drugs of all kinds.[20]

The person who, more than any other single figure in the 1960s, promoted LSD and other psychedelic drugs as the way to spiritual progress was Timothy Leary who died in 1996. Today most young people and most drug users have never heard of him. But for some years in the 1960s Leary was the guru of the spiritual quest through the use of drugs. It was he and his colleagues at the League for Spiritual Discovery who placed the use of psychedelic (or mind-expanding) drugs firmly within a religious framework. Leary has been misrepresented a good deal by his critics. He never claimed that drugs were an automatic gateway to mystical experience. At the same time his claim was quite extreme. He saw the LSD trip as the classic visionary voyage, and believed that the levels to which LSD leads people are those which have been called the confrontation of God. The LSD trip was for Leary the contemporary form of the mystical experience.

By the time that Leary was writing, the claim that drugs could aid spiritual development was widely known, and taken for granted by many. What was new in Leary was the centrality of LSD to his world view, and his suggestion that what conventional psychiatry described as psychosis, and conventional religion saw as irresponsibility, might well be more accurately seen as the resurgence of the quest for mystical experience which both had suppressed. It was Leary too who located 'ecstasy' at the heart of politics. According to Leary, the ecstatic process produced by fasting or yoga exercises can now be initiated by drugs. 'The drug induced ecstasis is now called the psychedelic experience.' He formed the League of Spiritual Discovery as a religion using psychedelic chemicals. Leary once distinguished low church and high church LSD users, with low church represented by Ken Kesey, acid rock and freak-outs, and high church by Watts, still very much the Anglican, ceremonialist, serene, aesthetic, even aristocratic.[21]

It was not difficult to ridicule Leary or to point to defects in his thought. Roszak spoke of his 'impenetrably occult narcissism'.[22] Both Huxley and Leary were the subject of fierce attack by a leading authority on eastern religions, the late Professor R C Zaehner. Zaehner first entered the drugs debate in 1957 when he included in his book *Mysticism Sacred and Profane* a critique of Huxley's claims about mescalin. He commented:

> The importance of Huxley's *Doors of Perception* is that in it the author clearly makes the claim that what he experienced under the influence of mescalin is closely comparable to a genuine mystical experience. If he is right . . . the conclusions . . . are alarming.[23]

Originally Zaehner took the view that drugs could only induce the lower types of mystical state – natural and monistic mysticism – and not theistic types. However, within two decades, Zaehner's alarm seemed to have declined, and in a study published in 1972, he wrote:

> I do not question that LSD can produce an almost unlimited expansion of consciousness, and that this may add a totally new, awesome and numinous aspect to life; nor do I question that LSD can deepen religious experience, if the desire to have done with self and all selfishness is there; nor does it seem wrong to me to use LSD or other psychedelic drugs as aids to meditation or even as substitutes for meditation.[24]

However, Zaehner remained one of the strongest critics of Timothy Leary and of the attempt to relate LSD experience to states of mystical awareness. Zaehner argued that there is no single 'mystical state' but rather a range of experiences in the religious literature of east and west which are described as 'mystical' in some sense. He rightly argued that much of the writing on drug-induced mysticism was unsophisticated and ignorant. For example, it is absurd to claim that LSD experience is at the same time one of 'cosmic consciousness' and of 'instant Zen' since the state of Nirvana is the exact reverse of cosmic consciousness. The quest for ecstasy and for what Jung termed 'inflation' was treated with great suspicion in the classical mystical tradition. Spiritual writers tend to stress sobriety, inner peace and the integration of mysticism into practical everyday life.

The concern with everyday life, and the emphasis on distinguishing religious experiences from religious life, was also a concern of the Indian spiritual teacher Meher Baba. Baba's involvement in the drug scene dates from a pilgrimage in 1965 which has been called, somewhat extravagantly, 'a pilgrimage which became a focal point for the downfall of the psychedelic fantasy'. Baba has been called 'the best non-acid authority available to compare the results of chemical stimulation of the deeper layers of being with those produced by techniques known and used throughout time by spiritual leaders'.[25]

Baba's critique is interesting and follows some general classical guidelines within both eastern and western mystical traditions. He warns of the danger of becoming attached to the experiences. Continued drug use for spiritual purposes, he argues, is superficial and adds to the deceptions of illusion. The search for God through drugs must end in disillusionment. The evidence does seem to support his view. However, what is at issue is not the character of the experience, aided or not aided by chemicals, but the relationship between spiritual experiences and spiritual life.

What kind of claims then can we make for drugs in relation to spirituality? First, it would seem illogical, and incompatible with an incarnational and sacramental theology, to deny that, in principle, chemical agents could be used to enhance religious experience. However, as with fasting, breathing exercises, methods of meditation, and other ascetical disciplines, it is necessary to distinguish aids and methods from the goal of the spiritual life. There is enough evidence that the use of drugs can awaken people to spiritual realities. There is not much evidence that, as a long-term component of religious discipline, drugs can be particularly useful.

> There seems to be no reason to deny (unless one makes a platonic dualism between mind and body) that the chemical changes in the body created by ascetic disciplines might indeed be artificially created by drugs. The difference obviously is that the second method will not flower out of a depth clarification of the self through discipline, for there can be no short cut to that.
>
> (Rosemary Ruether, 1970)[26]

Of course, most of the classical spiritual guides do not give attention to the use of drugs but some of their teaching on other issues is relevant to this question. For example, the author of *The Cloud of Unknowing* warns of forms of counterfeit contemplation in which the person is open to 'false lights and sounds'. St John of the Cross warns against reliance on experiences, and claims that 'apprehensions', even when given supernaturally, are a 'complete impediment to the attainment of spirituality'.

This conclusion connects with the view of many psychiatrists that drugs are 'agents which reveal but do not chart the mental regions'.[27] The danger of confusing spiritual enlightenment with ego-inflation is one which is ever-present within drug subcultures. It is a danger of which the mystics are only too well aware, and there are frequent warnings in these writers against 'false enlightenment'. The New Testament itself distinguishes the knowledge which 'puffs up' from the love which 'builds up', a clear expression of the danger of separating experience from praxis. It is a point made strongly by Allan Y. Cohen in his critique of the use of LSD for religious purposes.

> It was very clear that the psychedelic movement was taking a spiritual direction by 1963. It was inevitable, because people were encountering levels and alterations of consciousness which they couldn't explain by any psychological conception. The word 'consciousness' was suddenly discovered and was responsible for the link between chemical experience and religious experience. People discovered that

> spiritual figures, particularly in the east, talked about consciousness in the same way as western men talked about the search for God. The experience under these materials was sufficiently dramatic that, with the proper set and setting, you could be 100 per cent sure that you had experienced God. But the question which had to be faced was: *did* you experience God? There is no question that chemicals, and other forms of external manipulation (for example, fasting, flaggelation), can produce alterations of consciousness and religious experiences. If I stick you in a church and give you 500 microgrammes of LSD I will guarantee you a religious experience. (It might be of hell – but that's religious!)

But Cohen went on to question the value of the chemical approach on the grounds that it did not show positive fruit in terms of holiness of life.

> One of the fantasies we used to have is now demonstrably false. This is the belief that if you take enough psychedelic drugs, you will become holy, spiritually sophisticated, wise, expanded consciousness, love, will flow from you. It doesn't happen to work . . . Our attempts . . . failed not because of the quality of the people but because these results do not accrue from chemical-induced experience. You can't carry over even the profound experiences that you have. You can feel very loving under LSD, but can you exert that love to someone whom previously you didn't like? The long-range answer is No. It is almost beyond controversy. The controversy has now shifted into: Maybe it can get you started, but something else has to end it – one's own effort. But when you see the psychedelic leaders of the world, after a gorgeously mystical brotherhood love session, as they are coming down, having a bitter argument about who should wash the dishes, a sense passes through one that somehow sainthood has been missed.[28]

Drugs and despair

> I have made a decision. I am going to try to nullify my life.
> (The Velvet Underground)[29]
>
> Through ages man's desire
> To free his mind, to release his very soul,
> Has proved to all that live
> That death itself is freedom for evermore,
> And your troubled young life
> Will make you turn
> To a needle of death.
>
> (Bert Jansch, 1960s)[30]

For many people who use drugs, particularly those who use the opiates, there is no abiding sense of pleasure, ecstasy or enhanced consciousness, but a sense of despair and hopelessness. As Lindesmith pointed out fifty years ago, 'the average American addict is in fact a worried, troubled, and harried individual. Misery, alienation and despair, rather than pleasure and ecstasy, are the key features of his life'.[31] His words are true of many thousands of British addicts today. Of course, they are not peculiar in this respect, for there is a profound spiritual emptiness at the heart of our society, and drugs are closely related to this emptiness. Drugs expose it in a most dramatic and, at times, terrifying form, but they have not invented it. The role of priests and pastors, as well as lay Christians, in sharing this hopelessness and helping people see a way through it, is as urgent as it ever was. Pastoral care must always take the issues of despair with great seriousness. Perhaps the drug explosion will help us to understand something which has been present in our tradition for thousands of years, the truth of staying with the darkness in hope, with stability and faithfulness, remembering Bruce Kenrick's words, written about his work with heroin users in East Harlem in the early 1960s:

> . . . the church must suffer and be crucified with those it seeks to serve; and . . . it must keep on being crucified even though the nails bite deep and the hope of resurrection is obscure.[32]

Much of our ministry in the future, as in the past, will consist in the nurturing and sustaining of hope in the midst of unutterable pain and anguish.

How seriously do religious people take all this?

> Is there no one in the mainstream of the Christian clergy who troubles to ask – and I do not mean only rhetorically – why it is that so many Americans turn to the exotic cults and alien traditions we find among us?
>
> (Theodore Roszak, 1977)[33]
>
> Their lawlessness is self-confessed as is their anarchy . . . There may be a sensible case for the use of troops . . . Let it never be said that this government, through lack of determination, presided over the rapid growth of an alternative society.
>
> (Robert Key, MP, 1991)[34]

Roszak's question of twenty years ago, addressed to an American audience, is still relevant today and beyond the USA. The real failure of the Church in this whole area lies not in its inability to respond to crises, though that leaves much to be desired at times. It is rather that there has been a loss of perception and of insight, a failure to see the profound, often desperate spiritual yearning which is going on, and which sometimes, indeed often, finds its outlet in drugs. It would not be much of an exaggeration to say that a great deal of the drug use in the west is an expression of the confusion and perplexity in our culture about meaning and purpose in life, and about what it is to be human.

Ann Wright's study of Croydon noted that 'the Moslem community was alone in mentioning concern about the effects of drug abuse on the spirit'.[35] In the USA and parts of Britain, the Black Muslims have responded to the drug crisis by a powerful emphasis on local and global community. In a twelve-year follow-up of New York addicts, G E Vaillant noted that abstinence from drugs 'depends upon the addicts discovering gratifying alternatives'.[36] If this is true, then it would seem that one of the primary tasks facing all religious communities, hopefully working in a co-operative way, is the creation of what Roszak calls a 'healthy ecology of the spirit',[37] an environment in which access to God is possible, and in which harmful drug use becomes less necessary.

8

Politics, Policies and Pastoral Theology

> Drugs are dangerous because they are prohibited, not prohibited because they are dangerous . . . Our problem is not drugs but our drugs policy.
>
> (Dr John Marks, 1997)[1]
>
> One whole wing of social reformers has gone, it seems to me, altogether astray. They are preoccupied with relieving distress, patching up failures, reclaiming the broken down. All this is good and necessary. But it is not the social problem . . . It is no use giving opiates or stimulants to men whose daily regimen is unhealthy. It is no use devising relief schemes for a community where the normal relationships are felt to be unjust.
>
> (R. H. Tawney, 1912)[2]

The growth of illicit drug use, and the official and unofficial responses to it, can be compared to events in the life cycle of an ostrich. First, there is the burying of heads in the sand – no problem, no likelihood of one, no cause for panic, or indeed for action of any sort. But the reassurances against panic then give way to an explosion of panic. The ostrich begins to flap its wings in a state of panic – alarm about particular drugs, panic about doctors, and so on. Thirdly, the ostrich fights with its mate, and the warfare stage begins. The 'war on drugs', with its military metaphors, its language of escalation, conspiracy, and degeneration, which arises in this stage, is still with us. Finally, the ostrich lays an egg: the drug industry is born. Thousands of professional, well-paid drugs workers arrive in what is now an institutionalised network of activity, complete with briefcases, filofaxes and databases. Drug dependence becomes an acceptable field of study. Research institutes are set up, social workers, doctors and nurses enter the field, and a mountain of literature is produced about a population whom several years earlier most workers would not have touched with a bargepole.

It is necessary for pastors to understand the kinds of responses over the years which affect the pattern of drug use. Often responses to drugs are more harmful than the drugs themselves. Public responses and policies can hinder and impede as well as aid and strengthen pastoral work. It is therefore worth reflecting on each of these phases.

The head-in-the-sand phase can be illustrated by the general refusal or inability of the Ministry of Health, as it then was, throughout the 1960s to recognise the urgency of the trends to which even the Home Office had been trying to draw their attention. At national, local community and individual levels, the temptation to ignore warning signs and to pretend that all is well is a continuing danger. Political figures are still very resistant to change, or, in some cases, even to discussion about the possibility of change. A recent example was the statement by Nigel Evans, a shadow cabinet spokesman on drugs and co-chair of the All-Party Drug Misuse Group, that to set up a Royal Commission would amount to an endorsement of drug use![3]

The panic stage is particularly dangerous for it produces the very unbalanced, paranoid and often deranged reactions which its perpetrators ascribe to drugs. As Lester Grinspoon and James Bakalar commented:

> There is something very special about illicit drugs. If they don't always make the drug user behave irrationally, they certainly cause many non-users to behave that way.[4]

This stage shows most clearly that the responses to drug use can be more dangerous than the drugs themselves.

> Drugs are with us to stay. Fight them and they will grow ever more destructive. Accept them and they can be turned into non-harmful, even beneficial forces.
>
> (Dr Andrew Weil, 1972)[5]

Panic then has a tendency to lead to war. The military and authoritarian model has done incalculable damage to drug work, yet it seems to be the only model which many public figures know or understand, and its rhetoric is omnipresent; hence the use of words like 'war' and 'tsar'. Yet its dangers are clear for all to see. It replaces understanding by warfare. It despises informed debate, and tramples upon areas of complexity. It creates its own version of reality, and makes the problems it identifies worse. Sadly it is the warfare model which has dominated much British drug policy since the late 1960s, although many informed people warned that authoritarian and prohibitionist approaches would have disastrous results.[6]

Once the laying of the egg has occurred, and drug addiction has become an industry, the danger is that the actual drug user gets forgotten as the whole scene becomes bureaucratised and managerial. Once this process has occurred, there is the additional danger, and probability, that certain groups, with their own conventions and norms, dominate the scene, and the expression of alternative opinions becomes more difficult. A critical theological perspective is urgently needed here.

The international drugs traffic and the role of governments

There are, of course, international aspects here. For drugs are 'a currency in a vast economic system . . . an economy which stretches around the world'.[7] One writer on foreign affairs claims that 'governments themselves and the links they develop with major traffickers are the key both to the drug trafficking problem and to its solution'.[8] Certainly the USA has formed alliances with drug dealers who were anti-communist, and the role of the CIA in helping to bring about the cocaine explosion in American cities is well known. Many governments are involved in, or collude with, the drug trade. The study of the politics of international drugs traffic is a complex area, and much of the literature is unhelpful. For example, while there is evidence to support a link between drugs traffic and terrorism in some places, a good deal of the writing about this is highly anecdotal, weak on evidence, and ideologically geared to a cold-war mentality.[9]

Churches have, for the most part, been more concerned with caring for the casualties than with monitoring the international traffic. An exception to this is the Catholic Institute for International Relations, which has studied aspects of the question, but it needs to be on the agenda of all international departments of churches as well as of local churches which have an international awareness.[10] Pastoral care now has global dimensions.

Again, it is important that policies are studied within their wider European context. There is a European Monitoring Centre on Drugs and Drug Addiction based in Lisbon. The emergence of the European Union has led both to a sharing of ideas among the member states, and to the creation of new possibilities for the traffic. The free movement of members within the European Union has made life easier in some respects for dealers, while, since the collapse of the USSR, new routes have opened up. Much international drug-related activity by governments, including those within Europe, is concerned with the area of control of supply. Supply-side operations have had some success, but in general they simply shift the operational bases from one place to another.

A study in 1997 showed that in the UK two-thirds of government expenditure on drugs went on law enforcement and only one-third on prevention, education and treatment, while other studies have demonstrated the very high cost of law enforcement, including not only the control of drug circulation but insurance premiums, burglar alarms and so on.[11] The crucial British legislation is the Misuse of Drugs Act 1971 which classifies drugs under three classes: Class A includes heroin, cocaine, ecstasy, PCP (angel dust), and LSD; Class B includes amphetamines, barbiturates and cannabis; Class C includes some other stimulants, and the benzodiazepines. As mentioned above, most of the drug expenditure goes on enforcement of international and national controls. Enforcement costs a great deal and does not work very well. The cost of treatment is much less and treatment very often works.[12] This contrast alone has led many informed people to call for a policy change or at least a rethinking of current priorities.

As far as national and local churches are concerned, the issues of drug policy which demand careful and continuous attention are those which operate at national and local levels, and this must be based on close scrutiny, accurate knowledge and courageous reflection. A good deal has been said above about policy matters at the local level, but there are national aspects which need examination and, where possible, action, not least from churches and religious organisations.

Government strategy

The previous administration in 1995 launched what they termed a 'new' strategy on drugs which still needs looking at with care. The Labour Party in opposition welcomed this policy, and it is clear that the present government has no new strategy of its own, but is, as on many other issues, carrying on those inherited from the Conservatives. However, the Conservative strategy ended in March 1998. The Minister responsible has spoken recently of the need to move '*towards* a new drugs strategy' (my italics), and so we can assume that for the foreseeable future it will still be 'towards'.[13]

The key document of the present strategy is a 114-page Green Paper entitled *Tackling Drugs Together* (Cm 2678), published on 19 October 1994 as a consultation document, and then issued in a revised form as a White Paper on 10 May 1995. At the launch of the original document and strategy, the then Minister Tony Newton announced the provision of £8.5 million to support more than one hundred new local Drug Action Teams, and of 'an information and education campaign for young people'. He described this as 'a new emphasis in our approach', and admitted that 'some of the shock tactics that have been used in one or two earlier campaigns have not proved as effective as we would have liked'.[14] The admission that shock tactics have not worked is refreshing. In spite of the multiplication of disasters in urban social policy, it is still unusual for government ministers to admit that they were wrong, and this was as close to an admission as we are likely to get. Shock tactics did not work, as most of the government's advisors had warned them, and they may well have had the opposite effect to the one intended. Drug workers were warning of the danger of shock tactics as long ago as 1967. However, while there has been a certain shift away from such tactics, the present government seems still to be committed to the 'war on drugs' rhetoric in spite of much evidence of its failure. The Prime Minister still uses the language of the 'war on drugs'.[15]

The use of the word 'new' in 1994 was curious. Preventive work is at least thirty years old, and it is good that the government has now recognised its importance but it is very late in the day, and a lot of damage has already been done. It is important to say this not to score points but to recognise the reality that, after so much damage, true prevention is no longer possible in many instances. One cannot prevent what has already occurred, and so much drug work now is bound to be of a different kind. *The Guardian*, in an editorial on 20 October 1994, said that the government statement had come ten years too late: thirty years would have been more correct.

The most disappointing aspect of the strategy is the failure to see how drugs policy has itself helped to produce the present appalling situation. We never had illicit powder heroin, or criminal syndicates, in the UK drug scene until after 1968. The correlation between heroin/cocaine use and chronic unemployment is a post-1980s phenomenon. Britain has followed US urban policies (including drugs policies) in all those areas where they have most conspicuously failed. The late H. B. Spear, for many years head of the Home Office Drugs Inspectorate, said shortly before his death that British drugs policy had been 'an unmitigated disaster'. Now not only doctors and youth workers but senior police officers are saying this loudly and clearly. Until the damage due to policy is recognised, there will be no substantial improvement. There is therefore a need for churches to engage in policy issues on drugs as they have in other areas. In the USA, the Religious Coalition for a Moral Drugs Policy has brought together people from many faith traditions, and similar work is being done in Britain by the Drug Policy Review Group.[16]

One important change in central strategy has been the appointment of a senior advisor to the government to coordinate drugs policy, called by the curious term the 'drug tsar', a term which unites American and pre-revolutionary Russian rhetoric in a strange way. The idea comes from the USA where it reflects and reinforces the dominant concern with enforcement rather than with prevention or treatment. The appointment may lead to some new thinking, though it must be said that the experience of the equivalent official in the USA is not encouraging in this respect. One American authority on drug use, Dr Arnold Trebach, has compared the American drug tsar to the British monarchy – 'honoured but with no power'.[17] But it is too early to speculate on how the new official will affect policy.

The problem of funding

At the local level, there are many obstacles which those working with drug users need to be aware of. A persistent problem is that there is often no real needs assessment, and therefore a lack of proper funding. Adequate pastoral care cannot happen under present conditions without financial support, and there are major problems about funding in this area. Here local agencies, including churches, encounter the fragmentation and lack of systemic thinking of central and local government. The fact is that no one knows what is being spent and by whom, and while there is growing coherence at some levels, there seems to be a profound incoherence in funding. Area health authorities make sudden changes, with serious effects on local service provision, and in fact recent reductions in funding by health authorities have led to the collapse of some important work. Again, funds may move from one budget to another. In many areas 'community care' is little more than a euphemism for neglect, or is not understood by those whom it is meant to help. A study by the King's Fund in 1997 claimed that mental health services in London were close to collapse, and this inevitably affects drugs work. Projects can no longer obtain funding for juveniles and young adults who are at risk of addiction but have not been asssessed by a statutory social worker as needing moderately expensive hostel care. Many projects run hostels but can obtain funding only for chronically mentally sick people and those who are highly disruptive.

Since 1995 there have been serious cuts in provision in many areas – youth service, residential provision, health education co-ordinators (effectively abolished in 1993 through the ending of central support) and so on. Many projects in the prevention field have collapsed, or are in danger of collapse. In Tower Hamlets, for example, perhaps the most deprived borough in the UK, a number of innovative projects, including those working with Asian drug users, have disappeared through sudden cuts in health authority funding.[18] Often it is impossible to obtain funding for administration without which grant applications cannot be made in the first place. Often too drugs workers find that they have to be so concerned with funding that they are forced to neglect the needs of the young people for whom the project exists. Again, there are serious problems in the area of residential care with huge variations from one place to another. The Director of the Institute for the Study of Drug Dependence has rightly described rehabilitation as the Cinderella of drug services. One of the problems here is that of accelerating bureaucracy. One local authority procedure for consideration for rehabilitation presented the client with a sixteen-page form which took over thirty minutes to complete.

There are also the problems associated with the internal market and the resulting competitiveness between agencies. Groups invited to submit bids will find themselves in competition with other groups with whom they are supposed to be working in a co-operative way. The purchaser/provider split and the internal market has made collaborative work much more difficult, and has done incalculable harm to the work of care. However, it is clear that in many areas local action was ineffective and superficial prior to the introduction of these changes. A report from the Government's Social Services Committee in 1985 commented that few local authorities had 'much of a clue' about how to deal with drugs issues.[19]

Since the strategic changes of 1995, there is no doubt that there have been improvements – better local partnerships, more focused efforts, more commitment and involvement. The establishment of the Central Drugs Co-ordinating Unit has helped to overcome the haphazard approach of government departments. There are now 105 Drug Action Teams (DATs) in England, and 24 in Wales, Scotland and Northern Ireland, and in many areas groups known as Drug Reference Groups (DRGs), intended to reflect a wide range of local interest, have been set up. An independent study of the DATs by Middlesex University suggested that 60 per cent of DATs were broadly successful, although they were least successful in the area of allocation of resources. DATS need more strategic influence over funding.

Community care

The expression 'community care' was first used in the Report of the Royal Commission on the Law Relating to Mental Illness and mental deficiency in 1957. However, in practice it has become a euphemism for neglect, and as a result more mentally ill people now live on the streets. The 'community care' legislation has created other problems for drug work. Provision of accommodation involves assessment by a social worker. However, drug rehabilitation is often a low priority, and social service departments are often reluctant to spend money on long-term rehabilitation programmes. The report by the Social Services Inspectorate in 1995 was highly critical of five authorities which had no policy or strategy relating to drug and alcohol services.[20]

Of course there are many success stories, but the recent saga of 'care' is a sad one. There is a serious maldistribution of resources, much creative and innovative work, many experienced workers, and yet so much wastage of effort as government and local authorities spend money, establish more and more inquiries, employ more and more researchers, while in the process many lives are ruined or lost. It one of Britain's most spectacular areas of policy failure. As a Department of Health report said in March 1997:

> A lack of properly focused, accessible services for young people with potentially severe drug and poly-drug misuse problems represents a significant gap in service provision.[21]

The decision of the government, announced in January 1998, to change the present system of community care is overdue and welcome, but it remains to be seen what will replace the present system.

Variations in local drug policies

> Too much attention has been paid to increasing the number of drug users with whom services have contact without examining the impact of that contact. So far little attention has been paid to whether any benefit is conferred by this widely spread thin layer of provision.
>
> (Dr John Strang, 1996)[22]

There are significant variations in local drugs policies which have important effects on individuals and communities. Thus in 1992–3 more than one hundred addicts died in a fourteen-month period in Glasgow, almost all of them injecting heroin and temazepam. In Lothian, on the other hand, in the same period, deaths declined to 15–20 as a result of the policy of methadone treatment. Between 1988 and 1993 the practice of injecting declined dramatically among Edinburgh drug users from an estimate of 97 per cent to one of under 45 per cent, while HIV rates among drug users fell from 21 per cent to 8 per cent. When a new methadone prescribing service was established in Glasgow in 1994, it led fairly quickly to a reduction both in drug use and in sexual and injecting high-risk practices, and to an improvement in the health and social adjustment of the users.[23]

More generally, there is no doubt that needle and syringe exchanges have had dramatic effects on the spread of HIV and AIDS, reducing the incidence of the virus and preventing epidemic spread. Introduced experimentally in 1987, such exchanges spread quickly here to become an integral part of the framework of health-care delivery. Often, however, the provision of clean needles and syringes is in contrast to the lack of provision of clean drugs! The contrast between Britain and the USA here is quite dramatic, though there are also striking differences within the USA in relation to the presence of syringe exchanges.[24]

An ongoing question is that of the prescribing of heroin for addicts. There is a good deal of evidence that heroin prescribing has social advantages, and this was, of course, a major part of the rationale for such prescribing from the 1920s onwards. However, after the 1968 Act there was a strong hostility among a number of the psychiatrists at the new clinics, and after a study in 1976, there was a marked shift to oral methadone (although the authors of the study did not agree with the anti-heroin position).[25] In part of Merseyside, the return to heroin prescribing combined with provision of needles and syringes led quickly to a drop in the crime rate, a dramatic drop in HIV infection, and a decline in the numbers of new addicts.

Criminalisation and prohibition

> Penalties against possession of a drug should not be more damaging to an individual than the use of the drug itself; and where they are, they should be changed. Nowhere is this more clear than in the laws against possession of marijuana in private for personal use.
>
> (President Jimmy Carter, 1977)[26]
>
> We are doing many things to tackle the drugs problem. But let me say what we are not doing. We will not decriminalise, legalise or legitimise the use of drugs.
>
> (Jack Straw, MP, 1997)[27]

Finally, there is the issue of decriminalisation and legalisation. The terms are often used interchangeably, though strictly decriminalisation refers to the pragmatic decision to 'turn a blind eye' to what is still technically a criminal offence, while legalisation refers to a change in the law itself. In fact, a good deal of effective decriminalisation has already occurred in Britain. In Scotland, for example, small-scale cannabis possession is now roughly equivalent to a parking violation with a fixed penalty.

Those who argue for decriminalisation (and possibly for legalisation) point out that prohibition not only does not work, but actually makes the problems worse. Prohibition in Asia closed down the opium dens with the result that injecting heroin took over and led to the massive HIV epidemics which we now see in Thailand, Burma, south-west China, north-east India and Malaysia. On a national scale, a tremendous amount of time, energy and money is put into the enforcement of a law which most informed people, including many police officers, believe to be unworkable and unnecessary. That would be serious enough, but there is a more serious aspect. If the law is not only ineffective but leads to a worsening of the situation, this must raise questions about the law. The question about cannabis (for example) is therefore not 'How dangerous is this drug?' but 'Is the law relating to cannabis less or more dangerous than the drug itself?' The dilemma with which legislators are faced can be stated as follows. If the law is too lax, we get the problems we now have with alcohol. If it is too tight, then criminals move in.

The government's consultation document *Tackling Drugs Together* (1994) made no reference to harm reduction, though the final version (1995) did concede that the reduction of risks was necessary. However, the apparent reluctance to take harm reduction seriously is not encouraging.

A major part of our predicament is that there has been little if any new thinking at the official level in Britain about drugs policy for many years. It has been assumed that prohibition, war, control, is the answer, even though the evidence is overwhelming that this is not so.

In the Netherlands, a different approach has been followed for some time, an approach based on the concept of 'harm reduction' which I discussed earlier. While it has incited the wrath and outrage of other members of the European Community – President Chirac of France, for instance, called the Netherlands a 'narco-state' – the Dutch evidence is impressive and encouraging. For example, drug-related deaths in the Netherlands are among the lowest in the whole of Europe. Most such deaths are in the more repressive countries. Violent crime, much of which is drug-related, is massively higher in the USA than in the Netherlands. Moreover, the Netherlands has seen a decline both in addiction and in the numbers of people using cannabis, in contrast to both Britain and the USA. Again, 70–80 per cent of addicts in the Netherlands are known to the caring agencies, while 10–40 per cent is the norm in most other countries.

Dutch policy is based on three ideas. First, there is a legal separation of drug markets combined with an educational and health strategy. The possession of small amounts of drugs for personal use is not a criminal offence. Secondly, there is a stress on harm reduction. Thirdly is a political concept of 'normalisation', that is, the recognition that drug use is a normal part of life, and therefore the emphasis is on reducing use, containing and managing the damage done.[28]

Nor is Holland unusual. In Switzerland, an experiment of providing state-distributed heroin was found to reduce crime and to save money. The debate on policy reform will continue, and pastors need to make their views known.[29] It is, however, one of the oddities of human nature and of human institutions that methods which do not work and even make things worse are encouraged, while those which seem to be successful are pilloried. In other contexts, such an attitude would be described as psychotic and might be attributed to the effect of drugs. The lesson of history surely is that irrational behaviour does not depend upon drug use to induce it. It is all too common, and it makes pastoral care more difficult as well as more necessary.

It should be clear to everyone who is concerned with pastoral care of drug users that care is affected, helped or undermined, by policies. Sadly, however, not all carers do recognise this. It is important therefore for pastoral work not to neglect the crucial effect of policy. The limiting of the church's concern to issues of pastoral care and crisis management is seriously defective, and certainly does not fit well with the tradition of Anglican social thought and action, which, since the nineteenth century, has strongly emphasised the role of policy and legislation in shaping the course of people's lives. Pastoral theology cannot be restricted to ambulance work. In Peter Selby's words:

> To presume to care for other human beings without taking into account the social and political causes of whatever it is they may be experiencing is to confirm them in their distress while pretending to offer healing.[30]

References

Abbreviations used throughout the references and bibliography

Arch Gen Psych	*Archives of General Psychiatry*
Add Res	*Addiction Research*
BJ Add	*British Journal of Addiction*
BMJ	*British Medical Journal*
Bull Narc	*Bulletin of Narcotics*
IJDP	*International Journal of Drug Policy*
Int J Add	*International Journal of the Addictions*
ISDD	Institute for the Study of Drug Dependence
JAMA	*Journal of the American Medical Association*

Preface

1. Alfred R. Lindesmith, *Addiction and Opiates,* Chicago, Aldine Publishing Company [1947], 1968 edn, p 15.
2. Nils Bohr to his students, cited in Jacob Bronowski, *The Ascent of Man,* Boston, Little Brown and Company, 1973, p 334.
3. Simon Jenkins, *Evening Standard,* 16 February 1971; Derek Howard, *The Times Educational Supplement,* 18 September 1970.
4. Sue Mayo, in a talk given to youth workers in Bethnal Green in 1996.

Chapter 1

1. Lucretius, *De Rerum Natura.*
2. Cf 'Drugs are a menace to our society', former Prime Minister John Major, introduction to *Tackling Drugs Together,* Consultative Document, October 1994. While we know what he meant, the

statement is highly inaccurate. He could equally have said, 'Drugs are a blessing to our society.'

3. See H. Rolleston, 'Alcoholism in medieval England', *British Journal of Inebriety* 31:2 (1933) pp 33–49. On the historical relationship between church and pub see A. Tindal Hart, *The Parson and the Publican*, New York, Vantage Press, 1983.
4. See C. R. Snyder, *Alcohol and the Jews*, Yale Center Alcohol Studies, 1958; M. M. Glatt, 'Alcoholism and drug dependence among Jews', *BJ Add* 64 (1979), pp 297–304.
5. Data from the USA confirms that overdose from paracetamol (called Tylenol in the USA) is the main cause of hospitalisation for acute liver failure. See *New England Journal of Medicine*, 16 October 1997.
6. Cited in Hannah Steinberg (ed), *The Scientific Basis of Drug Dependence*, J. and A. Churchill, 1969, p 10.
7. See J. R. Reynolds, 'Therapeutic uses and toxic effects of cannabis indica', *The Lancet* 1 (1890), pp 637–8; A. D. Macdonald in *Nature* 147 (1941) p 168.
8. C. R. B. Joyce in Liam Hudson (ed), *Some Myths in Human Biology*, BBC Publications, 1972, p 74.
9. Franz Alexander and Sheldon Selesnick, *The History of Psychiatry*, New York, Harper and Row, 1966, p 14.
10. For an exception see James B. Ashbrook, 'Psychopharmacology and pastoral counselling: medication and meaning', *Journal of Pastoral Care* 49:1 (Spring 1995), pp 5–17.
11. See Oliver James, *Britain on the Couch: why we're unhappier compared with 1950 despite being richer. A treatment for the low serotonin society*, Century, 1997. On drugs and the brain see Heather Ashton, *Brain Function and Psychotropic Drugs*, Oxford University Press, 1992.
12. N. B. Eddy et al, 'Drug dependence: its significance and characteristics', *Bulletin of the World Health Organisation* 32:5 (1965), pp 721–733.
13. Tanzi, *Textbook of Mental Disease* (1909), cited by I. P. James in *British Journal of Criminology*, April 1969, p 108.
14. *Drug Addiction*, Report of the Interdepartmental Committee, HMSO, 1961, para 24.
15. The role of Bishop Brent indicates that Anglican clergy have been involved with the drug scene for some time. Since the 1980s I have been a visiting theologian at Bishop Brent House, the Anglican chaplaincy centre at the University of Chicago, a curious link which is worthy of a footnote!
16. For a valuable study of the early media panics about cocaine abuse see Marek Kohn, *Dope Girls: the birth of the British drugs underground*, Lawrence and Wishart, 1992. The panics centred on a number of clubs in Soho!

17. *Departmental Committee on Morphine and Heroin Addiction,* Ministry of Health, 1926. In the light of subsequent debates about funding and finance, it is amusing to note the statement on Page 1: 'The cost of this inquiry (including the printing of this Report) is estimated at £65. 5s. 6d.'
18. *Report to the United Nations by Her Majesty's Government of the United Kingdom and Northern Ireland on the Working of the International Treaties on Narcotic Drugs,* 1955, para 35.
19. J. Lockett (1952) cited in Adams, see below.
20. G. B. Adams, 'Patients receiving barbiturates in an urban general practice', *Journal of the College of General Practitioners* 12 (1966), pp 24–31.
21. William Burroughs, *The Naked Lunch,* Corgi, 1968, p 281.
22. On recent use of barbiturates see David Turner, 'Barbiturate use in Britain', *Druglink* 14 (Summer 1980), pp 6–7.
23. Peter Parish in *Drugs and Society* 7: 1 (April 1972), p 12.
24. On Prozac see Peter D. Kramer, *Listening to Prozac,* Viking Penguin, 1993. For an evangelical (and highly sympathetic) view see Clark E. Barshinger et al, 'The gospel according to Prozac', *Christianity Today,* 14 August 1995, pp 34–7. See also John Cornwell, *The Power to Harm: mind, medicine, murder on trial,* Viking Penguin, 1996; Mary Crowley, 'Do kids need Prozac?', *Newsweek,* 20 October 1997, pp 75–6; Caroline Daniel, 'Depressed? Just pop the Prozac', *New Statesman,* 19 September 1997, pp 18–19.
25. Sheldon Levine, *The Redux Revolution,* Morrow 1996; Michael D. Lemonick, 'The new miracle drug', *Time,* 23 September 1996, pp 51–59.
26. David E Smith and John Luce, *Love Needs Care,* Boston, Little Brown and Company, 1971, p 365.
27. *Jugs and Herrings,* Health Education Council Primary Schools Project, 1986; Hope UK study, cited in *Church of England Newspaper,* 27 June 1997.

Chapter 2

1. *Ministry of Health Report for the Year 1954,* Part 2, 1955.
2. P. H. Connell, *Amphetamine Psychosis,* Institute of Psychiatry and Chapman and Hall, 1958.
3. *Drug Addiction, Second Report of the Interdepartmental Committee,* HMSO, 1965, para 40.
4. Advisory Committee on Drug Dependence, *The Amphetamines and LSD,* HMSO, 1970. See Kenneth Leech, 'The junkies' doctors and the London drug scene in the 1960s: some remem-

bered fragments' in David K. Whynes and Philip T. Bean (ed), *Policing and Prescribing: the British System of Drug Control*, Macmillan, 1991, pp 35–59. On Petro see Kenneth Leech, 'John Petro, the junkies' doctor', *New Society*, 11 June 1981, pp 430–34, and Margaret Tripp, 'Who speaks for Petro?', *Drugs and Society* 3:2 (1973), pp 12–17. On Swan see Len Adams, 'He's taken over from Dr Petro', *The People*, 25 February 1968; 'Dr Swan pleads guilty to 13 charges', *Hackney Gazette*, 7 January 1969.

5. British Medical Association, *Report of the Working Party on Amphetamine Preparations*, 1968.
6. See, for example, D. S. Bell and W. H. Trethowan, 'Amphetamine addiction', *Journal of Nervous and Mental Diseases* 133 (1961), pp 489–96; L. G. Kiloh and S. Brandon, 'Habituation and addiction to amphetamines', *BMJ*, 7 July 1962, pp 40–43; J. A. Lago and T. R. Kosten, 'Stimulant withdrawal', *Addiction* 89 (1994), pp 1477–81; Ian Oswald and V. R. Thacore, 'Amphetamine and phenmetrazine addiction', *BMJ*, 17 August 1963, pp 427–431; D. G. Stewart and S. A. Brown, 'Withdrawal and dependency symptoms among adolescent alcohol and drug users', *Addiction* 90 (1995), pp 627–35.
7. Connell, op cit, p 71.
8. See Kiloh and Brandon, op cit. For a very thorough study of amphetamine problems in the USA see David E. Smith (ed), *Speed Kills: a Review of Amphetamine Abuse, Journal of Psychedelic Drugs* 2:2 (1969).
9. David Hawks et al, *The Abuse of Methylamphetamine*, MS, Addiction Research Unit, Institute of Psychiatry, 1969. A shortened version appeared in *BMJ*, 21 June 1969, pp 715–21.
10. See Andrew J. McBride et al, 'Amphetamine prescribing as a harm reduction measure: a preliminary study', *Addiction Research* 5:2 (1997), pp 95–112.
11. See Burton M. Angrist, 'Reported effects of "STP": the unreliability of hippies as reporters of drug effects', *BJ Add* 64 (1969), pp 23–4; S. H. Snyder, L. Faillace and L. Hollister, '2.5-dimethoxy-4-methylamphetamine (STP), a new hallucinogenic drug', *Science* 158 (1967), pp 669–70.
12. On MDMA see A. J. M. Forsyth, 'Ecstasy and illegal drug design: a new concept in drug use', *IJDP* 6:3 (1995), pp 193–209; Philip McGuire and Tom Fahy, 'Chronic paranoid psychosis after misuse of MDMA (Ecstasy)', *BMJ*, 23 March 1991, p 697.
13. On crack cocaine see Philip Bean (ed), *Cocaine and Crack: Supply and Use*, Macmillan, 1993; Richard Hammersley, 'The menace of the war on crack in Britain', *IJDP* 2:1 (1990), pp 28–30; J. Inciardi, 'Beyond cocaine: basuco, crack and other coca products', *Contemporary Drug Problems* 14:3 (1988), p 468ff; Harry Shapiro, *Crack: a briefing from the ISDD*, ISDD, August 1989; and

K. Verebeg and M. S. Gold, 'From coca leaves to crack: the effects of dose and routes of administration on abuse liability', *Psychiatric Annals* 18:9 (1988).

14. See *New York Times*, 28 March 1996.
15. Figures from Man Alive, BBC TV, 4 April 1978. See also M. W. Johns, 'Self-poisoning with barbiturates in England and Wales during 1959–74', *BMJ*, 30 April 1977, pp 1128–30; David Turner, 'Barbiturate use in Britain', *Druglink* 14 (Summer 1980), pp 6–7.
16. See Peter Parish in *Drugs and Society* 7:1 (April 1972) p 12; Forest S. Tennant, Jr, 'Complications of methaqualone-diphenhydramine (Mandrax) abuse', *BJ Add* 68 (1973), pp 327–30.
17. On benzodiazepines and related drugs see Jonathan Gabee (ed), *Understanding Tranquilliser Use: the role of the social sciences*, Routledge, 1991; Cosmo Hallstrom (ed), *Benzodiazepine Dependence*, Oxford, Oxford University Press, 1993; *Journal of Substance Abuse Treatment* 8:1–2 (1991), symposium on benzodiazepines; K. Koumijian, 'The use of Valium as a form of social control', *Social Science and Medicine* 15:3 (1981), pp 245–9. Peter Parish, 'The Prescribing of Psychotropic Drugs in General Practice', *Journal of the Royal College of General Practitioners* Vol 21, Supplement 4 (1971). On the abuse of these drugs in the care of the elderly see Michael Denham, *Medication for Older People*, Royal College of Physicians, 1997.
18. *Teaching About A Volatile Situation*, ISDD, 1980, p 1.
19. John Kilfeather and Viv Parker, *Creating Choices: a report on a group of long term solvent abusers*, City of Westminster Social Services Department, 1990, p 9.
20. On solvents see H. R. Anderson et al, 'An investigation of 140 deaths associated with volatile substance abuse in the United Kingdom 1971–1981', *Human Toxicology* 1 (1982), pp 207–221; John S. Cameron, *Solvent Abuse: a guide for the carer*, Croom Helm, 1988; Eve Merrill, *Glue Sniffing: a Guide for Parents and Professionals*, Birmingham, Pepar Publications, 1982; John Ramsey et al, 'Dangerous games: UK solvent deaths 1983–8', *Druglink* 5:5 (September-October 1990), pp 8–9; Justin Russell, 'Fuel of the forgotten deaths', *New Scientist*, 6 February 1993, pp 21–23; *Teaching About A Volatile Situation*, ISDD, 1980.

Chapter 3

1. Cited in Arnold Trebach, *The Heroin Solution*, Yale University Press, 1982, p 38.
2. John Jones, cited by I. P. James in *BJ Add* 62 (1967), p 391.

3. Isidor Chein et al, *Narcotics, Delinquency and Social Policy: The Road to H,* Tavistock Publications, 1964, p 372.
4. *Drug Addiction, Report of the Interdepartmental Committee,* HMSO, 1961, para 24.
5. *Report to the United Nations by Her Majesty's Government of the United Kingdom and Northern Ireland on the Working of the International Treaties on Narcotic Drugs,* 1964, para 40.
6. Ibid, 1965, para 37.
7. See Ros Coomber, 'How often does the adulteration/dilution of heroin actually occur?', *IJDP* 8:4 (1997), pp 178–86. See also Chapter Five, note 21.
8. William Burroughs, *Junkie,* 1966, p 12.
9. M. Hoffman in *Comprehensive Psychology* 5 (1964), p 262.
10. Isidor Chein et al, op cit, pp 218ff; P. T. D'Orban, 'Heroin dependence and delinquency in women', *BJ Add* 65 (1970), pp 67–78.
11. Lawrence Kolb in *Mental Hygiene* 9 (1925), p 609: 'the intensity of pleasure produced by opiates is in direct proportion to the degree of psychopathy of the person who becomes an addict'. See also his *Drug Addiction* (1962). See M. M. Glatt in C. W. M. Wilson (ed), *The Pharmacological and Epidemiological Aspects of Adolescent Drug Dependence,* Pergamon, 1968, p 172; and J. H. Willis, *Drug Dependence,* 1969, pp 71–2.
12. John B. Davies, *The Myth of Addiction,* Harwood Academic, 1992.
13. V. P. Dole and M. Nyswander, 'A medical treatment for diacetylmorphine (heroin) addiction', *JAMA* 193 (1965), p 646; M. Farrell et al, 'Methadone maintenance in opiate dependence: a review', *BMJ* 309 (1994), pp 997–1001.
14. M. Battersby et al, 'Horse trading: prescribing injectable opiates to opiate addicts: A descriptive study', *Drug and Alcohol Review* 11 (1992), pp 35–42; Richard Hartnoll et al, 'Evaluation of heroin maintenance in controlled trial', *Archives of General Psychiatry* 37 (1980), pp 877–84; Richard Hartnoll, 'Heroin maintenance and AIDS prevention: Going the whole way?', *IJDP* 4:1 (1993), pp 36–41.

Chapter 4

1. Dr Glatt said this at a public meeting in 1966.
2. Lord Sandford, House of Lords, 20 June 1967, col 1286.
3. *The Lancet,* 9 November 1963, p 989.
4. However, the earliest trace of cannabis use occurs in an archaeological find of hemp textile from China around 4000 BC. There is no hint of psychotropic use in these old scripts. See H. L. Li

and H. Lin, 'An archaeological and historical account of cannabis in China', *Economic Botany* 28:4 (1974), pp 437–47. It is also claimed that an Egyptian papyrus of the sixteenth century BC describes cannabis as a painkiller. See Philip Robson, *Forbidden Drugs*, Oxford University Press 1994, p 27.

5. See A. B. Toklas, *Cook Book*, Penguin, 1961 edn, p 306: 'haschich fudge'. She refers to 'canibus sativa' which she thinks may be difficult to obtain!
6. The main official reports on cannabis are those of the Indian Hemp Drugs Commission (1893), the Panama Canal Zone Military Investigation (1916–29), the Mayor of New York's Committee, the LaGuardia Report (1944), the Wootton Report in Britain (1968), and the Canadian Government's Commission of Inquiry, the Ledain Report (1970). On the National Commission on Marihuana and Drug Abuse and Nixon's response to its findings, see Dan Baum, *Smoke and Mirrors*, New York, Little Brown and Company, 1996.
7. C. D. J. Holman et al, *The Quantification of Drug Caused Morbidity and Mortality in Australia*, Canberra, Commonwealth Department of Community Services and Health, 1988.
8. The term 'amotivational syndrome' seems to have been used first by Dr David E. Smith, medical director of the Haight-Ashbury Free Medical Clinic in San Francisco. See David E. Smith, 'Acute and chronic toxiciity of marijuana', *Journal of Psychedelic Drugs* 2 (1968), pp 37–47; Christopher R. Creason and Morton Goldman, 'Varying levels of marijuana use by adolescents and the amotivational syndrome', *Psychological Reports* 48 (1981), pp 447–54.
9. Elizabeth Tylden, *Pot Is Not So Mild*, reprint from University College Hospital Students Magazine, 1969.
10. C. R. B. Joyce, letter in *New Society*, 30 January 1969, p 181.
11. See M. A. Plant, 'The escalation theory reconsidered: drug taking in an English town', *British Journal of Addiction* 68 (1973), pp 309ff, and his fuller study, *Drug Takers in an English Town*, Tavistock, 1975.
12. Elizabeth Tylden, *Cannabis Taking in England*, reprinted from the *Newcastle Medical Journal* 30:6 (1968).
13. O. Moraes Andrade, *Bull Narc* 16:4 (1964), p 27.
14. *Cannabis: Report by the Advisory Committee on Drug Dependence*, HMSO 1968. On the cannabis psychosis debate see Amanda J. Gruber and Harrison G. Pope, 'Cannabis psychotic disorder: does it exist?', *American Journal on Addictions* 3:1 (Winter 1994), pp 72–83; Roland Littlewood, 'Community initiated research: a study of psychiatrists' conceptualisations of 'cannabis psychosis', *Psychiatric Bulletin*, 1988, pp 486–89; Chris Ranger, 'Race, culture and "cannabis psychosis": the role of social factors in the con-

struction of a disease category', *New Community* 15:3 (April 1989), pp 357–69; Roland Littlewood and Maurice Lipsedge, *Aliens and Alienists: ethnic minorities and psychiatry*, Penguin, 1982, and 'Psychiatric illness among British Afro-Caribbeans', *BMJ* 296 (2 April 1988), pp 950–51.

For the data on cannabis, see, from an enormous list of possible sources: John Auld, *Marijuana Use and Social Control*, Academic Press, 1981; E. R. Bloomquist, *Marijuana: the Second Trip*, Collier Macmillan, 1971; J. D. P. Graham, *Cannabis Now*, Aylesbury, HM and M, 1977; Lester Grinspoon and J. B. Bakalar, *Marihuana: The Forbidden Medicine*, Yale University Press, 1993; Philip Robson, 'Cannabis', *Archives of Disease in Childhood* 77 (1997), pp 164–6; Michael Schofield, *The Strange Case of Pot*, Penguin, 1971; David E. Smith, 'The acute and chronic toxicity of marijuana', *Journal of Psychedelic Drugs* 2 (1968), pp 41–2; David E. Smith and Carter Mehl, 'Ananalysis of marijuana toxicity', *Clinical Toxicology* 3:1 (1970), pp 101–115; Andrew T. Weil et al, 'Clinical and psychological effects of marijuana in man', *Science* 162 (13 December 1968), pp 1234–42; N. E. Zinberg, 'On cannabis and health', *Journal of Psychedelic Drugs* 11 (1979), pp 135–44; N. E. Zinberg and A. Weil, 'Cannabis: the first controlled experiment', *New Society*, 16 January 1969, pp 84–6; Lynn Zimmer and John P. Morgan, *Marihuana Facts, Marihuana Fictions*, New York, Lindesmith Institute 1997.

15. Alison Halford, 'Making a hash of pot', *The Independent*, 31 May 1994.
16. The paper's correspondent Graham Ball claimed that 'cannabis did not become an issue until 1967' (*The Independent on Sunday*, 5 October 1997). In fact I argued the case for decriminalising cannabis in a lecture at the London School of Hygiene and Tropical Medicine on 7 March 1966 which received prominent coverage in *The Times* on 8 March and was fiercely attacked by Dee Wells in *The Sun* the following day.
17. The Rt Hon Ann Taylor, President of the Council, Address to Conference on 'Treatment Options: towards the 21st Century', Central Hall, London, 18 September 1997.
18. Timothy Leary, Ralph Metzner and Richard Alpert, *The Psychedelic Experience*, New York, University Books, 1965, p 14.
19. Lester Grinspoon and James B. Bakalar, *Psychedelic Drugs Reconsidered*, New York, Basic Books, 1981 edn, p 3.
20. Humphrey Osmond, *Annals of the New York Academy of Science* 66 (1957), p 418.
21. R. A. Sandison et al in *Journal of Mental Science* 100 (1954), p 498; Frank Lake, *Clinical Theology*, Darton, Longman and Todd, 1966.
22. Leary, Metzner and Alpert, op cit, p 135.

23. Ibid, p 11.
24. Herbert Marcuse, *An Essay on Liberation*, Penguin, 1972, pp 43–4.
25. *Druglink*, May-June 1991, p 4. On LSD see Sidney Cohen, 'LSD: the varieties of psychotic experience', *Journal of Psychoactive Drugs* 17:4 (1985), pp 291–6; Rick J. Strassman, 'Adverse reactions to psychedelic drugs: a review of the literature', *Journal of Nervous and Mental Disease* 172:110 (1984), pp 577–585.
26. For STP (2.5-dimethoxy-4-methylamphetamine) see Chapter Two on the methoxoy derivatives of amphetamine See also Burton M. Angrist, 'Reported effects of "STP": the unreliability of hippies as reporters of drug effects', *BJ Add* 64 (1969), pp 23–4; Michael Scott Beede, 'Phencyclidine intoxication', *Postgraduate Medicine* 68:5 (November 1980), pp 201–209.

Chapter 5

1. Les Kay and Chris Rowarth, 'Training about drug abuse', *SCODA Newsletter*, April-May 1985, p 12.
2. George Howarth, MP, Address to Association of Chief Police Officers, cited in *Daily Telegraph*, 17 July 1997.
3. Kenneth Leech, *Pastoral Care and the Drug Scene*, SPCK, 1970, Chapter Six, pp 59–79.
4. David M. Downes, *The Delinquent Solution*, Routledge 1966, p 135.
5. On the early Soho drug scene see Kenneth Leech as in note 3 above; and Harry Shapiro, *Waiting for the Man: the story of drugs and popular music*, Quartet Books, 1988.
6. See the reports from the Soho Project, the Blenheim Project, the Portobello Project and the Rink Project, especially *The Experimental Project with Unattached Young People*, Salvation Army Youth Project, 1968. These should be housed in one of the national youth work archives, and, if they are not, readers should bring pressure on youth work agencies to ensure that they are available.
7. Theodore Roszak, *The Making of a Counter Culture*, Faber, 1971 edn, p xii.
8. Laurie Taylor in *New Society*, 4 October 1973.
9. Roszak, op cit.
10. David E. Smith, lecture at St Anne's, Soho, 9 June 1970. See also David E. Smith et al, 'Love needs care: Haight-Ashbury dies', *New Society*, 16 July 1970, pp 98–101; and Kenneth Leech, 'The natural history of two drug cultures', *New Society*, 1 June 1972, pp 464–6.

11. See Kenneth Leech, 'Danger on the drug scene', *Daily Telegraph*, 8 December 1996. See also Chapter Eight, note 3.
12. David M. Downes, op cit, p 135.
13. On the social context of ecstasy see Matthew Collin and John Godfrey, *Altered States: the story of ecstasy culture and acid house*, Serpent's Tail, 1997.
14. Cited by David Alton, MP, House of Commons, 13 July 1984, col 1501.
15. On Grimethorpe see John Sweeney, 'Miners' children in the pits of heroin', *The Observer*, 6 October 1996; on Bolton see Brian Iddon, MP for Bolton South East, cited in *The Guardian*, 11 August 1997.
16. The above is a summary of *The Marigold Project Report on Female Commercial Sex Workers in Tower Hamlets*, 1997. The names of the sex workers have all been changed. For other work on drugs and prostitution see Lyn Matthews, 'Outreach work with female prostitutes in Liverpool' in Martin Plant (ed), *AIDS, Drugs and Prostitution*, Tavistock/Routledge, 1989; and Lyn Matthews. 'Outreach on the front line', *Druglink*, March-April 1993, pp 14–15.
17. On the situation in the USA see Christopher Jencks, *The Homeless*, Harvard University Press, 1994, pp 41–8.
18. See Jeremy Larner and Ralph Tefferteller, *The Addict in the Street*, Penguin, 1966.
19. John Marks, 'Chicago Revisited', *Community Care*, 18–24 September 1997, p 18.
20. On the early criminal groups see Alan Bestic, 'Now the big gangs are moving in', *Weekly News*, 9 March 1968.
21. On purity and adulteration see Ros Coomber, 'How often does the adulteration/dilution of heroin actually occur?', *IJDP* 8:4 (1997), pp 178–86; 'Vim in the veins – fantasy or fact: the adulteration of illicit drugs', *Add Res* 5 (1997), pp 195–212; and 'The adulteration of drugs – what dealers do, what dealers think', *Add Res* 5 (1997), pp 297–306.
22. Cited in *Druglink*, March-April 1993, p 15.
23. On 'crack' see Russell Newcombe, *Crack in Liverpool: a preliminary study of a group of cocaine smokers*, Liverpool, Maryland Centre, 1989. On the American crack scene see Fox Butterfield, 'Drop in homicide rate linked to crack's decline', *New York Times*, 27 October 1997; Craig Reinarman and Harry G. Levine (ed), *Crack in America: demon drugs and social justice*, University of California Press, 1997; Terry Williams, *The Cocaine Kids: the inside story of a teenage drug ring*, Addison Wesley, 1989, and *Crackhouse*, Addison Wesley, 1992. See also Chapter Two, note 13.
24. See *Drug Misuse in the North West of England*, Drug Misuse Research Unit, University of Manchester, and Sexual Health and

Environmental Epidemiology Unit, University of Liverpool, July 1996.

25. Standing Conference on Drug Abuse, *Annual Report*, 1975, p 1.
26. Harry Shapiro, op cit, p 1.
27. The comedian Carl Maxim called Gallagher's statement 'a classic case of the pothead calling the kettle crack'.

Chapter 6

1. Paul Simon, 'Bleecker Street', *Wednesday Morning 3AM.*
2. Don Browning, 'Practical theology and political theology', *Theology Today* 42:1 (April 1985), pp 15–42 (p 16).
3. Megan Jones of the Association for Prevention of Addiction, speaking at Conference on 'Treatment Options: towards the 21st Century', Central Hall, London, 18 September 1997.
4. Ann Wright, *Faith Communities in the London Borough of Croydon and Drug-Related issues,* Croydon Urban Industrial Mission Consultation Group, September 1996, p 18.
5. For an early account of work in these three areas see Kenneth Leech, 'The role of voluntary agencies in prevention and rehabilitation of drug abusers', *BJ Add* 67 (1972), pp 131–6.
6. E. Brecher, *Licit and Illicit Drugs,* Boston, Little Brown and Company, 1972, cited in *Druglink,* September-October 1990, p 10.
7. Peter G. Hammond in *Proceedings of the 30th International Congress on Alcoholism and Drug Dependence, Amsterdam 1972,* Lausanne, 1972, pp 43–6.
8. John DiIulio, Professor of Politics and Public Affairs, Princeton University, in *Sojourners,* September-October 1997, p 18.
9. Lyn Matthews, cited in *The Guardian,* 17 June 1992.
10. See John Strang et al, 'The better-travelled treatment tourist', *Druglink,* May-June 1996, pp 10–13; Michael Farrell et al, *A Review of the Legislation, Regulation and Delivery of Methadone in Twelve Member States of the European Union,* Brussels, European Commission, 1996; M. Gossop and M. Grant, *The Content and Structure of Methadone Treatment Programmes: a study in six countries,* Geneva, World Health Organisation, 1990.
11. Tim Rhodes et al, *Out of the Agency onto the Streets,* ISDD Research Monograph 2, 1991, pp 12–14.
12. See G. V. Stimson, 'Risk reduction by drug users with regard to HIV infection', *International Journal of Psychiatry* 3 (1991), pp 401–415; Tim Rhodes and Alan Quirk, 'Where is the sex in harm reduction?', *IJDP* 6:2 (1995), pp 78–82.
13. On outreach work in relation to drugs see *The Changing Face*

of Outreach, Report of the Second National Outreach Workers Conference, University of Cardiff, 13–16 September 1994. On harm reduction and HIV/AIDS see Ernst C. Buning, 'Innovative approaches to AIDS prevention among drug users', *IJDP* 2:6 (1991), pp 10–12; and Gerry V. Stimson, 'The future of UK syringe exchange', *IJDP* 2:2 (1990), pp 14–17.

14. Barbara Ward, 'The Rootless Adolescent in the London Scene', paper given at St Anne's House, Soho, 16 September 1969.
15. On detached work see Janet Batsleer, *Working with Girls and Young Women in Community Settings*, Aldershot, Arena, 1996; David Downes, 'In at the end', *Anarchy* 27 (May 1963), pp 131–44 (on the Teen Canteen); Michael Farrant and Howard Marchant, *Making Contact with Unattached Youth*, Manchester Youth Development Trust, 1971; George Goetschius and Joan Tash, *Working with Unattached Youth*, 1967; Kenneth Leech, *Keep the Faith Baby*, SPCK, 1973, and *Care and Conflict: leaves from a pastoral notebook*, Darton, Longman and Todd, 1990; and Mary Morse, *The Unattached*, Penguin, 1965.
16. Harry Shapiro, 'The crack report', *Druglink*, September-October 1994, pp 13–15.
17. *The Observer*, 15 November 1992.
18. The term 'Piccadilly junkie' seems to have first been used by Ian Pierce James, at the time medical officer of Brixton Prison, in 1969. See I. P. James, 'Delinquency and heroin addiction in Britain', *British Journal of Criminology* 9 (April 1969), p 122.
19. On Soho at this time see Jane Alexander, 'The Circus', *New Society*, 15 May 1969; John Hester, *Soho Is My Parish*, Lutterworth, 1969; Kenneth Leech, *Care and Conflict*, op cit; 'The drug subculture and the role of the priest', *Ministry*, Spring 1969, pp 19–26; 'The London drug scene', *Drug Dependence*, Institute for the Study and Treatment of Delinquency, September 1970, pp 20–27; 'The natural history of two drug cultures', *New Society*, 1 June 1972, pp 464–6; and *Scene W1: a report on pastoral work in Soho and the drug scene in 1969*, St Anne's Church, Soho, 1970; and Harry Shapiro, *Waiting for the Man*, op cit.
20. Eric Blakebrough, personal correspondence, 24 May 1997. For an account of Kaleidoscope see Eric Blakebrough, *No Quick Fix: a church's mission to the London drugs scene*, Marshall Pickering, 1996 edn.
21. See Mary Beasley, *Mission on the Margins*, Lutterworth, 1997.
22. I found Louise Dolan, *Reconsidering Pastoral Care: the recovering addict or alcoholic and the local church*, MA thesis, University of Nottingham, 1996, extremely useful on after-care. See also Frank Wilson, *Counselling the Drug Abuser*, Lakeland, 1973, p 65. An excellent pamphlet from an evangelical Christian perspective is

David Pott and Duncan Vere, *The Abuse of Drugs: a Christian View,* InterVarsity Press, 1975.

23. On AA and Twelve Step Programmes see David Berenson, 'Alcoholics Anonymous: from surrender to transformation', *Family Therapy Newsletter,* July-August 1987; Laird P. Bridgman and William M. McQueen, 'The success of Alcoholics Anonymous: locus of control and God's general revelation', *Journal of Psychology and Theology* 15:2 (1987), pp 124–31; Jeffrey L. Bullock, 'Public language, public conversion: critical language, analysis of conversion and the history of Alcoholics Anonymous', *St Luke's Journal of Theology* 31:2 (March 1988), pp 127–41; Mark Galanter, *Cults: faith healing and coercion,* Oxford University Press, 1989, Chapter Nine, 'Charismatic healing groups: the AA example' (pp 176–213); Klaus Makela et al, *Alcoholics Anonymous as a Mutual Help Movement: a study in eight societies,* Madison, University of Wisconsin Press, 1996.
24. On practical aspects of rehabilitation and after-care see A. Preston and A. Malinowski, *The Rehab Handbook: a user's guide to choosing and using residential services for people with drug or alcohol problems,* Dorchester, CADAS, 1993.
25. On some of the theological issues see Linda A. Mercadante, *Victims and Sinners: spiritual roots of addiction and recovery,* Louisville, Westminster/John Knox Press, 1996.
26. Ulrich Simon, *A Theology of Auschwitz,* Gollancz, 1967, p 127.
27. The word 'apophatic' is used in Eastern Christian thought for the dimension in theology which is beyond articulation. I use it here in a broader sense to refer to the dark, paradoxical, inarticulate and hidden elements of pastoral care.

Chapter 7

1. Kenneth Leech, 'Drugs, youth and spirituality', *New Fire* 2:1 (Spring 1972), pp 6–10. See also, for more detailed reflections on the issues raised in this chapter, Kenneth Leech, 'The hippies and beyond', *The Modern Churchman* 16 (October 1972), pp 82–92; and *Youthquake: spirituality and the growth of a counter-culture,* Sheldon Press, 1973, and Abacus, 1976.
2. Theodore Roszak, *The Making of a Counter-Culture,* Faber, 1971 edn, p 1.
3. Advertisement for British Youth for Christ, *Church of England Newspaper,* 15 August 1969.
4. Geoffrey Ostergaard in *Freedom,* 27 February 1962.
5. See 'Aleister Crowley Revisited', *Gandalf's Garden 3* (1968), pp 27–9.

6. See R. D. Laing, *The Politics of Experience and The Bird of Paradise*, Penguin, 1967; and 'Religious experience and the role of organised religion' in *The Role of Religion in Mental Health*, National Association for Mental Health, 1967, pp 51–8.
7. See Roszak, op cit, and my *Youthquake*, op cit. Roszak tends to bypass the psychedelic culture, mentioning the 'San Francisco renaissance' (p 164) but then devoting 14 pages to Timothy Leary. On the 1960s spiritual scene see Robert S. Ellwood, *The Sixties Spiritual Awakening*, New Brunswick, New Jersey, Rutgers University Press, 1994.
8. Caroline Coon, 'The Hippie and the Psychedelic Scene', MS, St Anne's Church, Soho, 1969.
9. On the Nine O'Clock service see Roland Howard, *The Rise and Fall of the Nine O'Clock Service*, Cassell, 1997.
10. Allan Y. Cohen, 'The journey beyond trips', *The ARE Journal* 3:4 (Fall 1968), pp 26–33, and *LSD and the Search for God*, Church Literature Association, 1973.
11. Jim Griffin, *Gandalf's Garden 3* (1968), p 12.
12. Roszak, op cit, p 82. See also Theodore Roszak, *Unfinished Animal*, Faber, 1977.
13. On New Age see John Drabe, *What Is the New Age Saying to the Church?*, Marshall Pickering, 1991; David Toolan, *Facing West from California's Shores: a Jesuit's journey into New Age Consciousness*, New York, Crossroad, 1987.
14. Timothy Leary, Ralph Metzner and Richard Alpert, *The Psychedelic Experience*, New York, University Books, 1965 p 11.
15. Colin MacInnes in *New Society*, 2 March 1967.
16. See William James, *The Varieties of Religious Experience*, Longmans Green, 1902, p 388. On Huxley see Aldous Huxley, *The Doors of Perception*, New York, Harper, 1954; *Heaven and Hell*, New York, Harper, 1956; Ian Thomson, 'Seeing the light', *The Independent Magazine*, 30 April 1994, pp 32–36. For the idea of 'artificial paradise' see Havelock Elis, 'Mescal: a new artificial paradise', *Contemporary Review* 73 (1898), pp 130–41.
17. Alan W. Watts, *This Is It*, 1960, p 17, and *The Joyous Cosmology*, 1962, p 17.
18. W. Pahnke and W. A. Richards, 'Implications of LSD and experimental mysticism', *Journal of Religion and Health* 5 (July 1966), pp 175–208.
19. Frank Lake, *Clinical Theology*, Darton, Longman and Todd, 1966, p xxii.
20. *Psychedelic Drugs and Krishna Consciousness*, Society for Krishna Consciousness, undated, probably 1969.
21. Timothy Leary in *Running Man* 1 (undated) p 14. See also Leary, Metzner and Alpert, *The Psychedelic Experience*, op cit; G. M. Weil,

Ralph Metzner and Timothy Leary (ed), *The Psychedelic Reader,* New York, University Books, 1965.

22. Roszak, op cit, 1971, p 64.
23. R. C. Zaehner, *Mysticism Sacred and Profane,* Oxford University Press, 1961, p 12.
24. R. C. Zaehner, *Drugs, Mysticism and Make Believe,* Collins, 1972, p 133.
25. *God In A Pill? Meher Baba on LSD and the High Roads,* 1966, p 2. For the reference to the pilgrimage see Allan Y. Cohen, 'The journey beyond trips', *The ARE Journal* 3:4 (Fall 1968), pp 26–33. See also Allan Y. Cohen, *LSD and the Search for God,* Church Literature Association, 1973. This pamphlet began as a talk given at St Anne's House, Soho, on 23 September 1969. For Cohen's approach, and his exposition of Meher Baba's teachings on drugs and spirituality see Allan Y. Cohen, *The Mastery of Consciousness,* Twickenham, Eel Pie Publishing, 1977; and Peter Marin and Allan Y. Cohen, *Understanding Drug Use,* New York, Harper and Row, 1971, pp 137–42.
26. Rosemary Ruether, *The Radical Kingdom: the western experience of messianic hope,* New York, Paulist Press, 1970, p 259. Ruether's words must be one of the first comments on psychedelic claims from a mainstream Christian theologian in a book on a different topic.
27. D. X. Freedom in *Archives of General Psychiatry* 18 (1968), p 345.
28. Allan Y. Cohen, *LSD and the Search for God,* op cit.
29. The Velvet Underground on their LP of the same name, issued in the late 1960s. The track is called 'Heroin'.
30. Bert Jansch's song 'Needle of Death' was one of the most popular songs about addiction, and was frequently sung by Jansch in Les Cousins and Bungies folk clubs in Soho. It is on his first LP entitled *Bert Jansch.*
31. Alfred R. Lindesmith, op cit, p 41.
32. Bruce Kenrick, *Come Out the Wilderness,* Fontana, 1965, p 155.
33. Theodore Roszak, *Unfinished Animal,* Faber, 1977, p 261.
34. Robert Key, MP, cited in *The Guardian,* 19th June 1991.
35. Ann Wright, *Faith Communities in the London Borough of Croydon and Drug-Related Issues,* Croydon Urban Industrial Mission Consultation Group, September 1996, p 18.
36. G. E. Vaillant, 'A twelve-year follow-up of New York narcotic addicts: 4. Some characteristics and determinants of abstinence', *American Journal of Psychiatry* 123 (1966), pp 573–84.
37. Roszak, op cit, 1977, p 43.

Chapter 8

1. John Marks, 'Chicago Revisited', *Community Care*, 18–24 September 1997, p 18.
2. J. M. Winter and D. M. Joslin (ed), *R. H. Tawney's Commonplace Book, Economic History Review Supplement 5*, Cambridge University Press, 1972, p 13.
3. Nigel Evans, MP, cited in *The Guardian*, 11 August 1997.
4. Lester Grinspoon and James Bakalar, *Marihuana: the Forbidden Medicine*, Yale University Press, 1993, p ix.
5. Andrew Weil, *The Natural Mind*, Boston, Houghton Mifflin, 1972, p 200.
6. *The Times*, in an editorial of 20 April 1964, warned that a repressive approach could be harmful. For warnings prior to the 1967 Dangerous Drugs Act see Brenda Jordan, Kenneth Leech and Judith Piepe, 'Drug addicts: authoritarian methods doomed to failure', letter in *The Guardian*, 4 February 1967; Kenneth Leech, 'Danger on the drug scene', *Daily Telegraph*, 8 December 1966; 'The drug scene', *Tribune*, 24 February 1966; 'Danger in the drug world', *Tribune*, 19 August 1966; 'Bad omissions in drugs bill', letter, *The Times*, 27 June 1967; and 'Dangerous drugs: a dangerous bill', *Tribune*, 7 July 1967.
7. *The Economist*, 8 October 1998, p 25.
8. Peter Dale Scott in Alfred W. McCoy and Alan A. Block (eds), *War on Drugs: Studies in the Failure of US Narcotics Policy*, Boulder, Westview Press, 1992, p 126.
9. See, for example, Richard Clutterbuck, *Terrorism, Drugs and Crime in Europe after 1992*, Routledge, 1990.
10. See *A Short Summary of CIIR's Drugs Trade and Development Programme*, Catholic Institute for International Relations, 1993.
11. See *Crime, Drugs and Criminal Justice*, Penal Affairs Commission, June 1997; and A. Wagstaff and A. Maynard, *Economic Aspects of the Illicit Drug Market and Drug Enforcement Policies in the UK*, Home Office Research Study 95, 1988.
12. *The Task Force to Review Services for Drug Misusers*, Department of Health, May 1996.
13. The Rt Hon Ann Taylor, President of the Council, Address to Conference on 'Treatment Options: towards the 21st Century', Central Hall, London, 18 September 1997. The White Paper *Tackling Drugs to Build a Better Britain*, issued on 27 April 1998, has been described as a 'new strategy' and as 'ground-breaking'. However, it offers no new understanding, but rather a continuation of earlier policies with a long-overdue emphasis on education and treatment. Whether this will be followed by adequate funding is not clear.

14. Cited in *The Times*, 20 October 1994.
15. The Rt Hon Tony Blair, Party Political Broadcast on BBC and ITA stations, 24 September 1997.
16. See Robert A. Sirico CSP, and Joseph Ganssle OFM (eds), *Reason, Compassion and the Drug War: A Statement by Religious Men and Women*, Washington DC, Religious Coalition for a Moral Drug Policy, 1990. The Coalition can be contacted at 3421 M Street NW, Suite 351, Washington DC 20007.
17. Cited in *The Guardian*, 11 August 1997.
18. See Polly Toynbee, 'Poverty by a thousand cuts', *The Independent*, 25 November 1996.
19. Social Services Committee, Recommendation 6, in *Misuse of Drugs*, HMSO, Cmnd 9685, 1985, p 5. See also *Inspection of Social Services for People who Misuse Alcohol and Drugs*, Department of Health, 1995.
20. Frances Rickford, 'No more room at the inn', *The Guardian*, 1 November 1995.
21. *Purchasing Effective Treatment and Care for Drug Misusers*, Department of Health, March 1997, p 23, summarising the Health Advisory Services Report.
22. John Strang et al, 'The better-travelled treatment tourist', *Druglink*, May-June 1996, pp 10–13.
23. See *Scottish Drugs Forum Bulletin*, February 1993; Judy Greenwood, 'Shared care with general practitioners for Edinburgh's drug users', *IJDP* 7:1 (1996), pp 19–22. The information on Glasgow after 1994 comes from the HIV and Addictions Clinical Directorate Resource Centre at Ruchill Hospital.
24. See G. V. Stimson et al, 'The future of UK syringe exchange', *IJDP* 2:2 (1990), pp 14–17; and G. V. Stimson and R. Lart, 'HIV, drugs and public health in England: new words, old tunes', *Int J Add* 26 (1991), pp 1263–77.
25. See R. L. Hartnoll et al, 'Evaluation of heroin maintenance in controlled trial', *Arch Gen Psych* 37 (1980), pp 877–84.
26. President Jimmy Carter, President's Message to Congress on Drug Abuse, August 1977, Strategy Council on Drug Abuse, Federal Strategy for Drug Abuse and Drug Traffic Prevention, Washington DC, US Government Printing Office, 1977, pp 66–7.
27. Jack Straw, MP, at the Labour Party Conference 1997, cited in *The Guardian*, 3 January 1998.
28. On Dutch policy see Henk Jan van Vliet, 'Drug policy as a managerial strategy: some experiences from the Netherlands', *IJDP* 1:1 (1989), pp 27–9; Craig Reinarman, 'The drug policy debate in Europe: the case of Califano versus the Netherlands', *IJDP* 8:3 (1997), pp 143–52.
29. For a good discussion of some of the issues in policy reform see Richard Stevenson, *Winning the War on Drugs? To Legalise or Not,*

Institute of Economic Affairs, 1994. The Drug Policy Review Group, PO Box 16548, London SE22 8ZT (0181 299 1295) will be interested to be in contact on how policy and pastoral care interact.

30. Peter Selby, *Liberating God*, SPCK, 1983, p 76.

Bibliography

General

Advisory Committee on the Misuse of Drugs, *AIDS and Drug Misuse, Part One*, HMSO, 1988.

Advisory Committee on the Misuse of Drugs, *AIDS and Drug Misuse, Part Two*, HMSO, 1989.

Advisory Committee on the Misuse of Drugs, *AIDS and Drug Misuse, Update*, HMSO, 1993.

Advisory Committee on the Misuse of Drugs, *Prevention*, HMSO, 1984.

Advisory Committee on the Misuse of Drugs, *Treatment and Rehabilitation*, HMSO, 1982.

T. H. Bewley, 'Recent changes in the pattern of drug abuse in the UK', *Bull Narc* 18:4 (1966), pp 1–13.

Richard Boxer and John Croston, *Drugtalk: the attitudes of young people to drugs*, St Albans, Drugcare, 1997.

Nicholas Dorn and Nigel South, 'Drug research and policy in Britain: a contemporary history', *IJDP* 1:1 (July–August 1989), pp 13–17.

Drug Addiction, Report of the Interdepartmental Committee, HMSO, 1961.

Drug Addiction, Second Report of the Interdepartmental Committee, HMSO, 1965.

Drug Misuse in the North West of England, Drug Misuse Research Unit, University of Manchester, and Sexual Health and Environmental Epidemiology Unit, University of Liverpool, July 1996.

N. B. Eddy et al, 'Drug dependence: its significance and characteristics', *Bulletin of the World Health Organisation* 32:5 (1965), pp 721–733.

Griffith Edwards and Carol Busch, *Drug Problems in Britain: a review of ten years*, Academic Press, 1981.

Cindy Fazey, *The Aetiology of Psychoactive Substance Use*, Paris, UNESCO, 1977.

M. M. Glatt et al, *The Drug Scene in Great Britain*, Edward Arnold, 1967.

Mannfred A. Hollinger, *Introduction to Pharmacology*, Taylor and Francis, 1997.

C. R. B. Joyce, 'Can drugs affect personality?' in Liam Hudson (ed), *Some Myths in Human Biology*, BBC Publications, 1972, pp 73–81.
Peter Laurie, *Drugs*, Penguin, 1967.
D. M. Louria, *Nightmare Drugs*, New York, Pocket Books, 1966.
Philip Robson, *Forbidden Drugs*, Oxford University Press, 1994.
Ronald K. Siegel, *Intoxication*, Simon and Schuster, 1990.
Andrew Tyler, *Street Drugs*, Hodder and Stoughton, 1995.
Jim Zacune and Celia Hensman, *Drugs, Alcohol and Tobacco in Britain*, Heinemann, 1971.

Opiates and cocaine

R. de Alarcon, 'The spread of heroin abuse in a community', *Bull Narc* 21:3 (1969), pp 17–22.
Philip Bean (ed), *Cocaine and Crack: supply and use*, Macmillan, 1993.
John B. Davies, *The Myth of Addiction*, Harwood Academic, 1992.
Nicholas Dorn and Nigel South (ed), *A Land Fit for Heroin*, Macmillan, 1987.
Paul Eddy et al, *The Cocaine Wars*, Century Hutchinson, 1989.
Kenneth Leech, 'The junkies' doctors and the London drug scene in the 1960s: some remembered fragments' in David K. Whynes and Philip T. Bean (eds), *Policing and Prescribing: the British System of Drug Control*, Macmillan, 1991, pp 35–59.
Alfred R. Lindesmith, *Addiction and Opiates*, Chicago, Aldine Publishing Company, 1947.
Justine Picardie and Dorothy Wade, *Heroin: chasing the dragon*, Penguin, 1985.
Harry Shapiro, 'The crack report', *Druglink*, September-October 1994, pp 13–15.
David E. Smith and G. R. Gay (eds), '*It's So Good, Don't Even Try It Once': Perspectives on Heroin*, Prentice-Hall, 1972.
John Strang and Michael Gossop (eds), *Heroin Addiction and Drug Policy: the British system*, Oxford Medical Publications, 1994.
Arnold Trebach, *The Heroin Solution*, New Haven, Yale University Press, 1982.
Terry Williams, *The Cocaine Kids: the inside story of a teenage drug ring*, Addison Wesley, 1989.
Terry Williams, *Crackhouse*, Addison Wesley, 1992.

Amphetamines, Sedatives and Tranquillisers

Advisory Council on Drug Dependence, *The Amphetamines and LSD*, HMSO, 1970.

P. H. Connell, *Amphetamine Psychosis,* Institute of Psychiatry and Chapman and Hall, 1958.

P. H. Connell, 'The use and abuse of amphetamines', *The Practitioner* 200 (1968), pp 234–43.

M. M. Glatt, 'The abuse of barbiturates in the UK', *Bull Narc* 14:2 (1962), pp 19–38.

David Hawks et al, 'The abuse of methylamphetamine', *BMJ,* 27 July 1969, pp 715–21.

O. J. Kalant, *The Amphetamines: Toxicity and Addiction,* University of Toronto Press, 1966.

P. D. Scott and D. R. Wilcox, 'Delinquency and the amphetamines', *BJ Add* 61 (1965), pp 91–27.

Cannabis and Psychedelics

Advisory Council on Drug Dependence, *The Amphetamines and LSD,* HMSO, 1970.

John Auld, *Marijuana Use and Social Control,* Academic Press, 1981.

E. R. Bloomquist, *Marijuana: The Second Trip,* New York, Glencoe Press, 1971.

Allan Y. Cohen, 'Psychedelic drugs and the student: educational strategies' in R. E. Horman and A. M. Fox (eds), *Drug Awareness,* New York, Discus Books, 1970, pp 442–56.

Allan Y. Cohen, 'Who takes LSD and why?', *New Society,* 11 August 1966, pp 226–8.

Sidney Cohen, *The Beyond Within,* New York, Athenaeum, 1970.

Sidney Cohen, *Drugs of Hallucination,* Secker and Warburg, 1965.

R. C. DeBold and R. C. Leaf (eds), *LSD, Man and Society,* Faber, 1969.

Lester Grinspoon, *Marihuana Reconsidered,* Harvard University Press, 1971.

Lester Grinspoon and James B. Bakalar, *Marihuana: The Forbidden Medicine,* Yale University Press, 1993.

Lester Grinspoon and James B. Bakalar, *Psychedelic Drugs Reconsidered,* New York, Basic Books, 1979.

Leo Hollister, *Chemical Psychosis: LSD and Related Drugs,* Springfield, Charles C. Thomas, 1968.

National Commission on Marihuana and Drug Abuse, *Marihuana, Signal of Misunderstanding,* Washington, US Government Publishing Office, 1972.

Michael Schofield, *The Strange Case of Pot,* Penguin, 1971.

David E. Smith, 'LSD and the psychedelic syndrome', *Clinical Toxicology* 2:1 (March 1969), pp 69–73.

David E. Smith (ed), *The New Social Drug,* Prentice-Hall, 1970.

Brian Wells, *Psychedelic Drugs,* Penguin, 1973.

Lynn Zimmer and John P. Morgan, *Marijuana Myths, Marijuana Facts: a review of the scientific evidence,* New York, Lindesmith Institute, 1997.

Sociological

Matthew Collin and John Godfrey, *Altered States: the story of ecstasy culture and acid house,* Serpent's Tail, 1997.

Crime, Drugs and Criminal Justice, Penal Affairs Commission, June 1997.

David M. Downes, *The Delinquent Solutio: a study in subcultural theory,* Routledge and Kegan Paul, 1966.

Charles E. Goshen, *Drink, Drugs and Do-Gooders,* New York, Free Press, and London, Collier-Macmillan, 1973.

Kenneth Leech, 'Danger on the drug scene', *Daily Telegraph,* 8 December 1966.

Kenneth Leech, 'The natural history of two drug cultures', *New Society,* 1 June 1972, pp 464–6.

Martin Plant (ed), *AIDS, Drugs and Prostitution,* Tavistock/Routledge, 1989.

Martin Plant and Moira Plant, *Risk Takers: alcohol, drugs, sex and youth,* Sage Publications, 1995.

Irvine Welsh, *Trainspotting,* Secker and Warburg, 1993.

Irvine Welsh, *The Acid House,* Vintage, 1995.

Jock Young, *The Drug Takers,* Paladin, 1971.

E. M. Schur, *Narcotic Addiction in Britain and America,* Tavistock, 1963.

Penal and Policy Issues

W. F. Deedes, 'Drugs: why a blanket ban is the worst solution', *Daily Telegraph,* 15 December 1992.

Drug Prevention Initiative Annual Progress Report 1995–6, Home Office, 1997.

Health Advisory Service, *The Substance of Young Needs,* HMSO, January 1996.

Tim Murphy, *Rethinking the War on Drugs: drugs in Ireland,* Cork University Press, 1996.

Tackling Drug Misuse: a Summary of the Government's Strategy, Home Office, 1985.

Tackling Drugs Together, HMSO, 1995.

The Task Force to Review Services for Drug Misusers, Department of Health, 1996.

Arnold S. Trebach and Kevin Zeese, *Drug Prohibition and the Conscience of Nations,* Washington, Drug Policy Foundation, 1990.

BIBLIOGRAPHY

David K. Whynes and Philip T. Bean (eds), *Policing and Prescribing: the British System of Drug Control*, Macmillan, 1991, pp 35–59.

Pastoral Ministry

Eric Blakebrough, *No Quick Fix: a church's mission to the London drugs scene*, Marshall Pickering, 1996 edn.

Louise Dolan, *Reconsidering Pastoral Care: the recovering addict or alcoholic and the local church*, MA thesis, University of Nottingham, 1996.

John Frykman, *A New Connection: a problem-solving approach to chemical dependency*, Berkeley, Regent Press, 1992.

Dianne Hammersley, *Counselling People on Prescribed Drugs*, Sage Publications, 1995.

Anne Jamieson, Alan Glanz and Susanne McGregor, *Dealing with Drug Misuse: crisis intervention in the city*, Tavistock, 1984.

Bruce Kenrick, *Come Out the Wilderness*, Fontana, 1965

Kenneth Leech, *Care and Conflict: leaves from a pastoral notebook*, Darton, Longman and Todd, 1990.

Kenneth Leech, 'The drug subculture and the role of the priest', *Ministry*, Spring 1969, pp 19–26.

Kenneth Leech, 'The Soho crusaders and the ostrich', *The Guardian*, 11 May 1983.

Susanne McGregor et al, 'Paradigms and practice in drug services in England', *IJDP* 3:2 (1996), pp 16–17.

Gerald G. May, *Addiction and Grace*, Harper San Francisco, 1988.

Rowdy Yates, *If It Weren't for the Alligators*, Manchester, Lifeline Publications, 1992.

Spirituality

Allan Y. Cohen, 'Youth, mysticism and the search for God', *Crucible*, May 1970, pp 72–83.

John Drane, *What Is The New Age Saying to the Church?*, Marshall Pickering, 1991.

Harvey D. Egan, 'Christian mysticism and psychedelic drug experience' in *Studies in Formative Spirituality* 5:1 (February 1984), pp 33–41.

R. D. Laing, *The Politics of Experience and The Bird of Paradise*, Penguin, 1971.

Kenneth Leech, 'Drugs, youth and spirituality', *New Fire* 2:1 (Spring 1972), pp 6–10.

Kenneth Leech, 'The hippies and beyond', *The Modern Churchman* 16 (October 1972), pp 82–92.

Kenneth Leech, *Youthquake: spirituality and the growth of a counter-culture*, Sheldon Press, 1973, and Abacus, 1976.
Linda A. Mercadante, *Victims and Sinners: spiritual roots of addiction and recovery*, Louisville, Westminster/John Knox Press, 1996.
Michael S. Northcott, *The New Age and Pastoral Theology: towards the resurgence of the sacred*, Contact Monograph 22, 1992.
David Toolan, *Facing West from California's Shores: a Jesuit's journey into New Age Consciousness*, New York, Crossroad, 1987.
R. C. Zaehner, *Drugs, Mysticism and Make-Believe*, Collins, 1973.

Educational

Heidi Baker and Martin Caraker, *Do It Yourself: the process of developing a drugs information service for children*, Home Office Drugs Prevention Initiative, 1995.
Chill Out: the Ravers' Guide, Mersey Drug Training and Information Centre, 1992.
Ian Clements et al, *Taking Drugs Seriously: a manual of harm reduction education on drugs*, Heathwise, 1990.
Nicholas Dorn and K. Murji, *Drug Prevention: a review of the English language literature*, Institute for the Study of Drug Dependence, 1992.
P. A. O'Hare et al, *The Reduction of Drug Related Harm*, Routledge, 1992.
Skills for the Primary School Child: The World of Drugs, TACADE, 1995.

Treatment

L. E. Hollister, 'Treatment outcome: a neglected area of drug addiction research', *Drug and Alcohol Dependence* 25 (1990), pp 175–7.
Paul Lockley, *Counselling Heroin and Other Drug Users*, Free Association Books, 1995.
Klaus Makela et al, *Alcoholics Anonymous as a Mutual Help Movement: a study in eight societies*, Madison, University of Wisconsin Press, 1996.
The Task Force to Review Services for Drug Misusers, Department of Health, May 1996.

For references, bibliographies and details of other resources, the best source is the Library of the Institute for the Study of Drug Dependence, 32 Loman Street, London SE1 0EE (0171 928 1211 or 0171 803 4720).

Some Useful Addresses

Other useful literature and advice can be obtained from the following:

ADFAM (Aid for Addicts and their Families), 5th Floor, Epworth House, 25 City Road, London EC1Y 1AA (0171 638 3700).

Hope UK, 25 Copperfield Street, London SE1 0EN (0171 928 0848).

Institute for the Study of Drug Dependence, 32 Loman Street, London SE1 0EE (0171 928 1211 or 0171 803 4720).

National Drugs Helpline, 0800 776600.

Release, 388 Old Street, London EC1 V 9LJ (0171 729 9904).

Re-Solv, 30a High Street, Stone Staffs, ST15 8AW (01785 817885).

TACADE (The Advisory Council on Alcohol and Drug Education), 1 Hulme Place, The Crescent, Salford M5 4QA (0161 745 8925).

Index